McDOUGAL, LITTELL
Spelling

Dolores Boylston Bohen

Assistant Superintendent
Fairfax County Public Schools
Fairfax County, Virginia

Mary Johanna Lincoln Huycke

Elementary Teacher and Reading Specialist
Fairfax County, Virginia

4
AQUA LEVEL

 **McDougal, Littell & Company**
Evanston, Illinois

New York • Dallas • Columbia, SC

recycled paper

Objectives

- to teach the spelling of **words** as well as the spelling of sounds
- to stress the recognition of **structural** similarities as well as phonetic similarities
- to strengthen **associative** and **visual memory**
- to reinforce the **three modes of learning:** visual, auditory, and kinesthetic

Organization

Each lesson presents a word list that demonstrates one spelling pattern or generalization. The list is followed by three types of activities:

Practice the Words—three activities that require students to examine and write the words on the spelling list

Build Word Power—an activity that extends the application of words on the spelling list in a broader language arts context

Reach Out for New Words—two activities in which students work with new words that follow the spelling pattern

CONSULTANTS FOR THIS TEXT

Georgene G. Albert, Teacher, Pine Tree Independent School District, Longview, Texas
Carol Ashby, Teacher, Irvine Unified School District, Irvine, California
Naomi Engstrom, Teacher, Ukiah Unified School District, Ukiah, California
Lura M. Hoover, Teacher, Lakeland Community School Corporation, Milford, Indiana
Andrew L. Olson, Teacher, School District of Chetek, Chetek, Wisconsin
Mildred Seco, Teacher, North Fork School District, Glen Morgan, West Virginia
Deborah Siegler, Teacher, Jefferson Public Schools, Jefferson, Wisconsin
Wanda Travis, Teacher, Grant School District, Maysville, West Virginia
Win Yapp, Teacher, Scotts Valley Unified Elementary School District 408, Scotts Valley, California

Acknowledgments
Daily Mirror Newspaper, Ltd.: For "My Thoughts" by Sara Gristwood, which first appeared in the *Daily Mirror's Children's Literary Competition*; copyright © 1969. Lescher & Lescher, Ltd.: For "Since Hanna Moved Away" from *If I Were In Charge Of The World. . .and Other Worries* by Judith Viorst, published by Atheneum; copyright © 1981 by Judith Viorst. Marian Reiner: For "Growing Up" from *The Little Hill* Poems & Pictures by Harry Behn; copyright © 1949 by Harry Behn, copyright © renewed 1977 by Alice L. Behn, all rights reserved.

ISBN 0–8123–8578–0

Copyright © 1994 by McDougal, Littell & Company
Box 1667, Evanston, Illinois 60204
All rights reserved. Printed in the United States of America.

3 4 5 6 7 8 9 10 – WMW – 98 97 96 95 94

Contents

A Writer's Journal

Spelling Is for Writing

Imagine that you need to write about a play at your school. What would happen if you could not spell any of the words that you wanted to write?

You learn to spell in order to write. You write to express your feelings and ideas. This book will help you improve both your spelling and your writing. The more you practice both skills, the better speller and writer you will become.

One fun way to practice writing is to keep a journal. A journal is a notebook in which you write about your thoughts and feelings. You can write whatever comes to mind.

Plan now to keep a journal throughout the year. Write in your journal often. On some days you might write only a sentence or two. On other days you may write several pages. Here are some ways you can use your journal. You can

- tell about your feelings
- remember important events in your life
- describe what you have seen or imagined
- react to a poem or story you have read

Spelling and Your Journal

When you write in your journal, you may want to use words that you do not know how to spell. Do not stop writing. Instead, write the words as you think they should be spelled. When you are finished, look up the correct spellings in the dictionary. Keep a personal list of the words that give you trouble. You can refer to this list when you need to write the words in the future.

Getting Started

Here's an idea for your first journal entry. Finish the sentence "I feel _____ today because . . ."

Building a Personal Word List

What Is a Personal Word List?

You will use your spelling book to learn how to spell many words. You will also learn important ideas about how words are spelled in our language. In this way, the spelling book helps you become a better writer. There will be times, however, when you misspell a word or need to write a word that you do not know how to spell. These words can go on a special list called a personal word list. This list will contain words that you want to learn.

Words for your personal list can come from anywhere. Many of the words will come from your writing; others may come from books you read. Here are other places you might discover words:
- stories and poems you write
- readings in content areas such as science or social studies
- signs and advertisements

How to Keep a Personal Word List

Your personal words should be kept in a special place. You might want to write the words in the back of your journal or in a special notebook. It is important to keep your list handy so that you can add words to it and refer to the list easily.

As you collect words, notice the kinds of spelling mistakes you make. Think about the way the words are spelled. Are any of the words similar to words you know how to spell? Are they made up of spelling patterns you have studied? Noticing similarities can help you remember how words are spelled.

Making Words Your Own

Making a word your own means that you can use the word correctly in your writing. To do this, you will need to know what the word means and how to spell it. A dictionary can help you with the meaning and spelling. However, you will want to develop a way of learning to spell words. One method you can use is on page 7.

How to Spell a Word

Each week you will be learning to spell a new list of words. You will also be learning words from your personal list. You will need a system—or strategy—for studying these words. One way to learn to spell a word is explained below. You can use it as you prepare for your weekly spelling test and as you learn to spell words on your personal list.

1. Look at the word.

2. Say the word.

3. Spell the word aloud.

4. Copy the word.

5. Picture the word in your mind.

6. Cover the word and write it.

   Check for mistakes. If you have made a mistake, repeat steps 1 through 6.

Silent e words with the ending ing

vote + ing =		voting
slide + ing =		sliding
trade + ing =		trading
serve + ing =		serving
curve + ing =		curving
share + ing =		sharing
score + ing =		scoring
snore + ing =		snoring
shine + ing =		shining
invite + ing =		inviting
lose + ing =		losing
refuse + ing =		refusing
surprise + ing =		surprising
promise + ing =		promising
bounce + ing =		bouncing

1. What is the last letter you see in the word **vote**? ___

2. What is the last letter you hear in the word **vote**? ___

3. The words in the first column have a last letter that cannot be heard. What is that silent letter? ___

4. What ending was added to make the words in the last column? _____

5. The letters **a**, **e**, **i**, **o**, and **u** are **vowels**. Is the first letter of the ending **ing** a vowel? _____

6. What letter was dropped from each word before **ing** was added? ___

> When a word ends with **silent e**, drop the **e** before you add an ending that begins with a vowel.

Practice the Words

A Write the spelling words that complete these sentences.

1. Who keeps _____ the ball against the house?

2. We will be _____ dessert soon.

3. Whom is Michelle _____ to the party?

4. Rosa is _____ more points than Bill.

5. We will be _____ for a club president tomorrow.

6. Ben is _____ his apple for Sarah's grapes.

7. The police officer was _____ her flashlight into the dark alley.

8. The runner is _____ into second base.

9. Thank you for _____ your popcorn with me.

10. Ken keeps _____ to return my sweater, but he forgets.

11. Our baseball team was _____ the championship game.

12. The horse kept _____ to obey its rider.

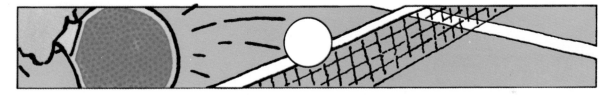

The **base form** of a word is the word before any changes have been made.

B Unscramble the base form of each spelling word and write it. The first letter has been given to help you. Then write the **ing** form of each word.

1. tenivi   _i_____   _____

2. sproime   _p_____   _____

3. cunobe   _b_____   _____

4. senhi   _s_____   _____

5. fuseer   _r_____   _____

6. sprusire   _s_____   _____

7. creuv   _c_____   _____

8. neros   _s_____   _____

9

C Add the missing vowels to complete each spelling word. Then write its base form.

1. r _e_ f _u_ s _i_ n g   *refuse*

2. s __ r p r __ s __ n g   _____

3. v __ t __ n g   _____

4. s h __ r __ n g   _____

5. s l __ d __ n g   _____

6. p r __ m __ s __ n g   _____

7. s __ r v __ n g   _____

8. c __ r v __ n g   _____

9. l __ s __ n g   _____

10. t r __ d __ n g   _____

11. s n __ r __ n g   _____

12. s c __ r __ n g   _____

Build Word Power

Writing

Write a sentence to answer each question. Use the **ing** form of the word in parentheses.

1. What are the boys doing outside?   (bounce)

_____

2. What kind of weather are we having today?   (shine)

_____

3. Whom is Mark asking to his party?   (invite)

_____

4. How are the Tigers doing in the game?   (lose)

_____

5. What are we doing for Jan's birthday?   (surprise)

_____

voting	serving	scoring	inviting	surprising
sliding	curving	snoring	losing	promising
trading	sharing	shining	refusing	bouncing

New Words

prepare   guide
prove   behave
escape   frame
dare   dine

Reach Out for New Words

A Write the **ing** form of each new word.

1. _____

2. _____

3. _____

4. _____

5. _____

6. _____

7. _____

8. _____

B Each sentence below tells about the actions of a person or animal. Write the **ing** form of the new word that describes these actions.

1. The park ranger is helping the lost campers find their way out of the woods.   *guiding*

2. The lion is sneaking out of his cage. _____

3. Grace is challenging Pam to swim across the lake. _____

4. The Wilsons are having roast beef, baked potatoes, and a salad. _____

5. The students are sitting quietly in the classroom. _____

6. Paula is cutting pieces of wood to fit around her oil painting. _____

7. Anne is jogging every evening to get ready for the race. _____

8. The suspect's plane ticket is showing that he was out of town when the store was robbed. _____

11

Silent e words with the ending ly

love + ly = lovely
like + ly = likely
lone + ly = lonely
live + ly = lively
late + ly = lately
wise + ly = wisely
wide + ly = widely
nice + ly = nicely
safe + ly = safely
sure + ly = surely
brave + ly = bravely
close + ly = closely
loose + ly = loosely
complete + ly = completely
sincere + ly = sincerely

1. The words in the first column end with what silent letter? ___
2. What ending was added to make the words in the last column? _____
3. The letters **a**, **e**, **i**, **o**, and **u** are vowels. The other letters are **consonants**. Does the ending **ly** begin with a consonant or a vowel? _____
4. Was the **silent e** dropped from each base word before the ending **ly** was added? _____

When a word ends with **silent e**, do not drop the **e** before you add an ending that begins with a consonant.

A Use each clue to find a spelling word that fits in the puzzle.

Across

2. nearly
6. a closing for a letter
8. full of energy
10. expected to happen
11. not long ago
12. not tightly

Down

1. over a large area
3. without any doubt
4. in a kind way
5. with courage
7. totally
9. in a smart way

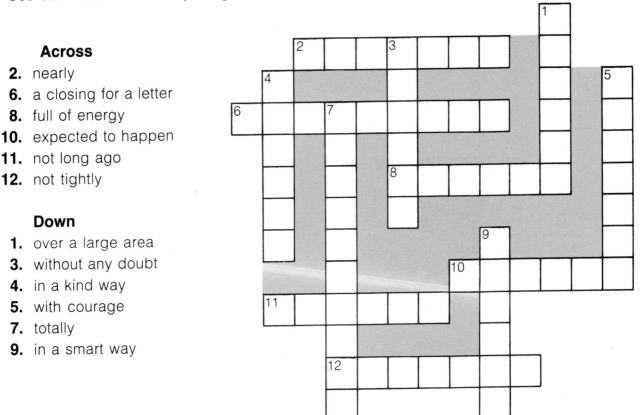

Proofreading

B Read this book report. Five of the underlined words are mis-spelled. Cross out the misspelled words. Write them correctly on the lines.

The Black Stallion is <u>surely</u> the best book I have ever read. It is about a boy who is lost in a storm at sea. He gets <u>safly</u> to a <u>lovley</u> desert island. It is not <u>likely</u> that anyone will find him. He <u>bravley</u> tries to make the island his home, but he is <u>lonly.</u> Then he meets a beautiful black stallion. They become friends and watch over each other as <u>closely</u> as brothers. The boy becomes <u>completly</u> happy in his island home.

1. _____   4. _____

2. _____   5. _____

3. _____

Dictionary

Words in the dictionary are listed in **alphabetical order**. When the first letter of two words is the same, the second letter is used to put them in alphabetical order. Sometimes you will need to use the third, fourth, or another letter to put the words in alphabetical order.

plan

plane

plate

C Write each group of words in alphabetical order.

1. nicely   _____

    safely   _____

    wisely   _____

    bravely   _____

    widely   _____

    sincerely   _____

    surely   _____

2. lively   _____

    completely   _____

    likely   _____

    lonely   _____

    loosely   _____

    lovely   _____

    closely   _____

    lately   _____

Build Word Power

Writing

Your spelling words can be used to write about people and the things they do. For example, read the following idea and story.

Idea: a firefighter rescuing people from a burning building

Story: The firefighter *bravely* went into the burning building. It was *likely* that people were inside. They had to be brought out *safely*. He *wisely* put on a mask because the building was *completely* filled with smoke.

Choose one of the story ideas below and write a story using as many spelling words as possible.

a movie star winning an award   a camper seeing a bear
a person stranded on an island   a racer coming in second

_____

_____

_____

_____

lovely	lively	widely	surely	loosely
likely	lately	nicely	bravely	completely
lonely	wisely	safely	closely	sincerely

New Words

strange	separate
secure	immediate
rare	entire

Reach Out for New Words

A Find the **ly** form of a new word that fits in each shape.

1.

4.

2.

5.

3.

6.

Write the **ly** form of the new word that matches each meaning.

1. totally _____

4. in a safe way _____

2. not together _____

5. not very often _____

3. in an unusual way _____

6. right now _____

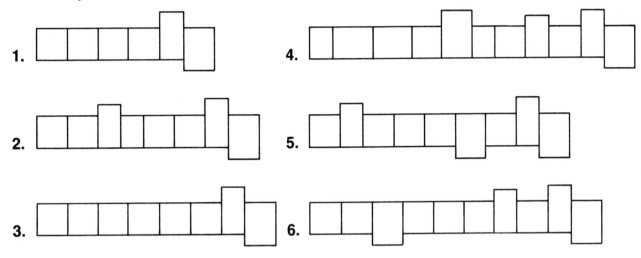

Writing

B Use each new **ly** word in a sentence.

1. _____

2. _____

3. _____

4. _____

5. _____

6. _____

care + ful = careful
use + ful = useful
hope + ful = hopeful
peace + ful = peaceful
waste + ful = wasteful
grace + ful = graceful
plate + ful = plateful
age + less = ageless
tire + less = tireless
taste + less = tasteless
change + less = changeless
score + less = scoreless
shape + less = shapeless
sleeve + less = sleeveless
home + less = homeless

A **suffix** is an ending added to a word to change the way the word is used.

1. The words in the first column end with what silent letter? ___
2. What suffix meaning *full of* or *having*
   has been added to the first seven words? _____
3. What suffix meaning *without* has been added to the next eight words? _____
4. Do the suffixes begin with a vowel or a consonant? _____
5. Was the final **silent e** dropped from
   each base word when the suffix was added? _____

When a word ends with **silent e**, do <u>not</u> drop the **e**
   before you add an ending that begins with a consonant.

Practice the Words

A Use each clue to find a spelling word that fits in the boxes. The **silent e** has been given to help you.

1. having a use; helpful

2. forever young

3. does not easily become tired

4. having hope

5. cautious

6. without a place to live

7. not clumsy

8. not at war

9. throws away things that can still be used

10. having no flavor

11. having no shape

12. a 0—0 game

13. always the same

14. without sleeves

B Find the misspelled word in each group. Then write the word correctly.

1. tireless
   changless
   hopeful

   _____

2. wakeful
   wasteful
   ageles

   _____

3. homeless
   hopeful
   platful

   _____

4. tasteless
   carefull
   shapeless

   _____

5. usful
   noiseless
   peaceful

   _____

6. wasteful
   tireless
   sleevless

   _____

C Write the spelling word that tells about each person or thing.

1. Bobby threw away a good pair of sneakers because they were dirty. Bobby is ___. _____

2. That dancer moves well to the music. He is very ___. _____

3. This meat needs salt and pepper. The meat is ___. _____

4. Karen thinks her picture may win a prize in the contest. She feels very ___. _____

5. Jenny has mowed the lawn, trimmed the bushes, and she doesn't need to rest yet. Jenny is ___. _____

6. This old bathing suit is baggy and loose. It is ___. _____

7. No one has crossed home plate in the baseball game. The game is ___. _____

8. There is never any trouble in our town. It is very ___. _____

9. Lisa ate a big dish of spaghetti and meatballs. She ate a ___. _____

10. A stray dog is looking for a place to live. He is ___. _____

Build Word Power

Words that have opposite meanings are called **antonyms.**

Write the spelling word that is the antonym, or opposite, of each word below.

1. thrifty _____   6. reckless _____

2. flavorful _____   7. useless _____

3. old _____   8. clumsy _____

4. shapely _____   9. hopeless _____

5. warlike _____   10. changing _____

18

careful	peaceful	plateful	tasteless	shapeless
useful	wasteful	ageless	changeless	sleeveless
hopeful	graceful	tireless	scoreless	homeless

New Words

price	sense
force	shame
defense	bone

Reach Out for New Words

A Find the **ful** or **less** form of the six new words in this puzzle. Some of the words may overlap. Circle each word and write it.

1. _____
2. _____
3. _____
4. _____
5. _____
6. _____

Writing

B Rewrite each sentence to make it more exact. Add the word in parentheses. The first one is done for you.

1. A mother tiger protects her cubs.   (defenseless)

   A mother tiger protects her defenseless cubs.

2. Fish are easy to eat.   (boneless)

   _____

3. Ms. Williams kept her jewels in a safe.   (priceless)

   _____

4. What caused this forest fire?   (senseless)

   _____

5. The mayor's speech convinced us to clean up the river.   (forceful)

   _____

6. Bob regretted his actions.   (shameful)

   _____

dream
speak
meat
cream
least
beneath

head
bread
thread
ahead
meant
weather

break
great
steak

1. What two letters do you see in every word? ___ ___

2. In how many words do the letters **ea** sound like **ee** in the word **see**? _____

3. In how many words do the letters **ea** sound like the **e** in the word **ten**? _____

4. In how many words do the letters **ea** sound like **a** in the word **ape**? _____

Many words are spelled with the letters **ea**.
The letters **ea** have different sounds.

Practice the Words

A Write the spelling words that complete these sentences.

1. I had a _____ and a baked potato for dinner.

2. Today's _____ will be rainy and cool.

3. Use blue _____ to hem your jeans.

4. Potatoes grow _____ the ground.

5. I practice the piano at _____ one hour every day.

6. Dad picked up vegetables, bread, and _____ at the grocery store.

7. Do you _____ when you are sleeping?

8. A police officer will _____ to our class about bicycle safety.

9. This football helmet does not fit my _____.

10. The baker sold fresh _____ and cakes at the fair.

11. Carol ran _____ of me in the race.

12. I _____ to buy Jim a birthday card, but I forgot.

Proofreading

B Cross out the misspelled words on these signs. Write the words correctly.

On Sale!

Bread	39¢
Meet	$2.29
Cheese	75¢
Round Staek	$1.89
Ice Creme	89¢

Local Bulletins

Local runner sure to braek state record

May 14 Mayor Reed to speek on home safety

May 26 Marvello the Grate to perform at carnival

Detour ahed

Watch Your Hed

FOOD

1. _____   5. _____

2. _____   6. _____

3. _____   7. _____

4. _____   8. _____

C Print the spelling word that fits in the shape and rhymes with the clue word.

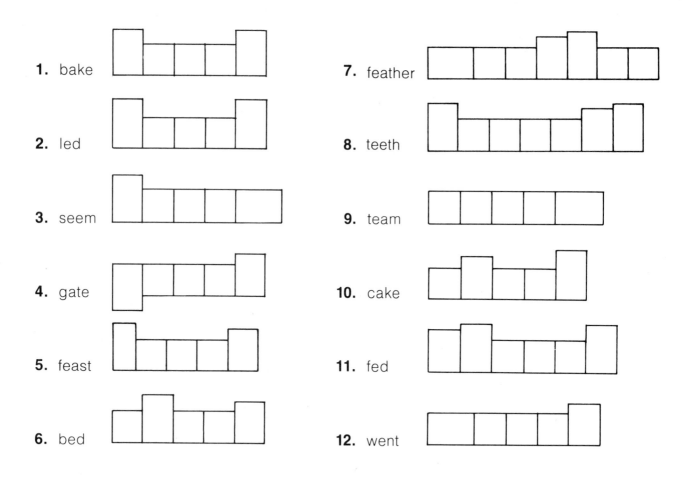

1. bake

2. led

3. seem

4. gate

5. feast

6. bed

7. feather

8. teeth

9. team

10. cake

11. fed

12. went

Build Word Power

An **analogy** is a special way of showing how words go together. Look at the first pair of words in each row. In what way do these words go together? Write a spelling word that makes the second pair of words go together in the same way as the first pair.

1. **glove** is to **hand**   as   **hat** is to   _head_

2. **balloon** is to **pop**   as   **glass** is to   _____

3. **beans** is to **vegetable**   as   **pork** is to   _____

4. **knit** is to **yarn**   as   **sew** is to   _____

5. **hamburger** is to **bun**   as   **jam** is to   _____

6. **last** is to **first**   as   **behind** is to   _____

7. **dog** is to **bark**   as   **person** is to   _____

dream	cream	head	ahead	break
speak	least	bread	meant	great
meat	beneath	thread	weather	steak

New Words

eager	treat
treasure	already
instead	peak
stream	feather

8. **bad** is to **terrible**   as   **good** is to   _____

9. **biggest** is to **smallest**   as   **most** is to   _____

10. **cereal** is to **milk**   as   **coffee** is to   _____

11. **frightening** is to **nightmare**   as   **pleasant** is to   _____

12. **say** is to **said**   as   **mean** is to   _____

Reach Out for New Words

A Words are printed in three directions in this puzzle. → ↓ ↘
Find the eight new **ea** words. Circle each word and write it. The first letter
of each word has been given to help you.

```
c  t  e  a  g  e  r  s
d  b  x  l  z  v  f  t
j  f  k  r  w  b  q  r
s  t  e  e  n  p  m  p
t  r  e  a  s  u  r  e
r  e  g  d  t  l  m  a
e  a  k  y  r  h  q  k
a  t  h  g  j  v  e  s
m  f  l  d  n  h  p  r
c  i  n  s  t  e  a  d
```

1. 𝑒 _____
2. 𝑡 _____
3. 𝑖 _____
4. 𝑠 _____
5. 𝑡 _____
6. 𝑎 _____
7. 𝑝 _____
8. 𝑓 _____

Writing

B Choose five of your new words. On another sheet of paper, write a riddle for
each. Give two clues for each riddle. See if a friend can guess the word and
write it correctly.

Example: Clue 1: used for sewing
               Clue 2: rhymes with **bread**   _thread_ _____

23

oil
boil
soil
foil
spoil
broil
coin
join
point
joint
choice
voice
noise
moisture
avoid

1. What two letters do you see in every word? _____
2. Are these letters usually at the beginning,
   in the middle, or at the end of the word? _____

Many words are spelled with the letters **oi**.
These letters are usually found in the middle of a word.

Writing

A Write the spelling word that completes each phrase.

1. _____ of a pencil

2. _____ for the garden

3. _____ the water

4. five cent _____

5. a scratching _____

6. _____ our club

7. a sore _____

8. food may _____

9. aluminum _____

10. second _____

11. talk in a low _____

12. grease and _____

Choose four phrases and use each in a sentence.

1. _____

_____

2. _____

_____

3. _____

_____

4. _____

_____

B Look at each word. If it is spelled correctly, draw a 🙂 . If it is misspelled, write the correct spelling.

1. koin _____

2. join _____

3. voice _____

4. noice _____

5. soil _____

6. briol _____

7. choise _____

8. moischure _____

9. joint _____

10. foil _____

11. avoyd _____

12. point _____

Dictionary

The two words at the top of each page in the dictionary are called **guide words**. The guide word on the left tells you the first word on the page. The guide word on the right tells you the last word on the page. All the words on the page are listed in alphabetical order between the two guide words.

guide word · guide word

load · mast

load ═══════════

mast ═══════════

C The word pairs below are guide words. What spelling words would go on each page? Write them in alphabetical order.

1. author   **crack**

_____

_____

_____

_____

_____

2. flower   **money**

_____

_____

_____

_____

3. night   **promise**

_____

_____

_____

4. sail   **water**

_____

_____

_____

Build Word Power

Write funny answers for these clues. Write the two rhyming spelling words that go in each pair of blanks.

1. pour water into grease   _spoil_ the _oil_

2. glue two halves of a dime together   _____ the _____

3. tryouts for a glee club   a _____ _____

4. to cook dirt   _____ the _____

5. the sharpest part of your elbow   the _____ of the _____

oil	foil	coin	joint	noise
boil	spoil	join	choice	moisture
soil	broil	point	voice	avoid

Reach Out for New Words

A Each number in this code stands for one letter of the alphabet. Decode each word in the paragraphs below. Print the correct letter on the blank above each number.

j	q	f	m	a	i	s	c	g	r	x	b	z	h	u	p	d	k	o	y	t	e	l	w	v	n
1	2	3	4	5	6	7	8	9	10	11	12	13	14	15	16	17	18	19	20	21	22	23	24	25	26

1. The sailors __ __ __ __ __ __ __ __ at the end of a perfect day of
             10 22 1 19 6 8 22 17

sailing. The wind had come up early in the morning. First the sailors had untied the

ropes that held the boat. Then they had __ __ __ __ __ __ them on the deck,
                                          8 19 6 23 22 17

and __ __ __ __ __ __ __ the sails. The boat had skimmed across the water
     14 19 6 7 21 22 17

all day. Tonight the sky was so clear the sailors thought they could see a planet or an

__ __ __ __ __ __ __ __ among the stars.
5 7 21 22 10 19 6 17

2. Janet was very __ __ __ __ __ __ __ __ __ __ __ __. A little
                        17 6 7 5 16 16 19 6 26 21 22 17

plant had spoiled her vacation. She hadn't known that the three-leaved vine was

__ __ __ __ __ __ ivy! Now, instead of going swimming, she had an
16 19 6 7 19 26

__ __ __ __ __ __ __ __ __ __ __ with the doctor!
5 16 16 19 6 26 21 4 22 26 21

B Write the new **oi** word that fits each meaning.

1. a tiny planet _____

2. a planned meeting _____

3. something harmful _____

4. lifted up _____

5. was very happy _____

6. wound in circles _____

Contractions

they	+ will	=	they'll
they	+ are	=	they're
here	+ is	=	here's
she	+ is	=	she's
there	+ is	=	there's
you	+ would	=	you'd
they	+ would	=	they'd
we	+ would	=	we'd
does	+ not	=	doesn't
would	+ not	=	wouldn't
will	+ not	=	won't
has	+ not	=	hasn't
have	+ not	=	haven't
could	+ not	=	couldn't
should	+ not	=	shouldn't

1. The words in the last column are **contractions**.
Each contraction is made from how many words? _____

2. Were any letters left out when the words were joined? _____

3. In each contraction an **apostrophe** takes the place of one or more letters.
Write an apostrophe. ___

A contraction is made from two words. When the
two words are joined, an **apostrophe** (') takes
the place of one or more letters.

The contraction **won't** is special. When the words **will** and **not**
are put together, changes are made in both words.

will + not = won't

A Write the contractions in alphabetical order in the first column. Then answer the questions to complete the chart.

	Contraction	What two words does it stand for?	What letter(s) does the apostrophe (') replace?
1.	couldn't	could not	o
2.			
3.			
4.			
5.			
6.			
7.			
8.			
9.			
10.		they will	
11.			
12.			
13.			o (also change **will** to **wo**)
14.			
15.			

B Write the contraction for each pair of words. Each contraction should fit in the boxes. An apostrophe fills one box.

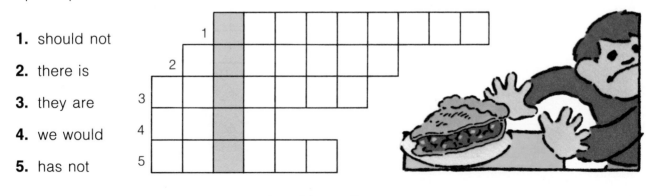

1. should not

2. there is

3. they are

4. we would

5. has not

What contraction is hidden in the colored boxes? _____

C Find each pair of words that can be made into a contraction. Then write the contraction.

1. Here is the shoe I could not find yesterday.

_____

2. They will have a cookout on Sunday if it does not rain.

_____

3. Sara will not bake a cake if you would prefer cookies.

_____

4. My parents have not found a house they would like to buy.

_____

5. It would not surprise me if Joan has not been told.

_____

Build Word Power

Complete this word chain using the words shown below. Begin by finding the word that ends with the letter **I** and fits in the seven spaces in that row. Count one space for the apostrophe.

they'd
they'll
won't
doesn't
hasn't
haven't
we'd
you'd

On another sheet of paper, try to make your own word chain.

they'll	she's	they'd	wouldn't	haven't
they're	there's	we'd	won't	couldn't
here's	you'd	doesn't	hasn't	shouldn't

New Words

when's	where's
they've	it'll
mustn't	o'clock
who'll	

Reach Out for New Words

A The words that form each new contraction fit in the sets of lines and letters. The contractions fit in the boxes. Write the words and contraction that go with each set of lines and boxes. Remember to count one box for the apostrophe.

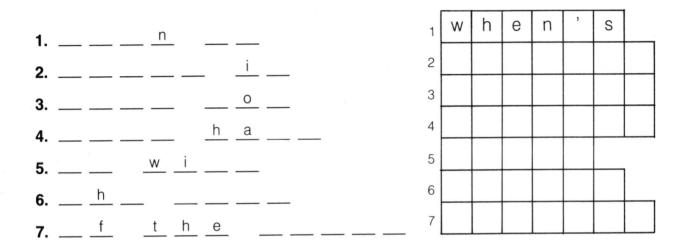

1. __ __ __ n __ __ __

2. __ __ __ __ __ i __

3. __ __ __ __ __ o __

4. __ __ __ __ h a __ __

5. __ __ w i __ __

6. __ h __ __ __ __ __

7. __ f __ t h e __ __ __ __ __

Grid:
1. w | h | e | n | ' | s

B Rewrite each sentence. Replace the underlined words with a contraction.

1. <u>They have</u> already finished the game.

_____

2. Joe <u>must not</u> tell his sister about the surprise party.

_____

3. I think <u>it will</u> reach ninety degrees today.

_____

4. Sam will meet you at four <u>of the clock</u>.

_____

5. <u>Who will</u> win the five-mile race?

_____

chief
niece
piece
field
fierce
shield
brief
believe
cashier

receive
ceiling

eight
weigh
neighbor
reindeer

1. The letters **i** and **e** are in each of these words.
   In how many words do you see the letters **ie**? _____

   In how many words do you see the letters **ei**? _____
2. Look at the words **receive** and **ceiling**.
   Do you see the letters **ei** or **ie** after the letter **c**? _____
3. Find the four words in which you hear the
   sound of the letter **a**. Do you see **ei** or **ie**? _____

This rhyme will help you spell words that have the letters **i** and **e**.

> **i** before **e**
> except after **c**
> or when sounded like **a**
> as in **neighbor** or **weigh**

A Write the spelling words that complete these sentences.

1. The _____ gave me 59¢ in change.

2. The baseball game was postponed because of a muddy _____.

3. There is a _____ missing from this jigsaw puzzle.

4. I like to _____ mail from my pen pal.

5. The _____ of police spoke to the other officers.

6. The grocer will _____ those apples on the scale.

7. Mrs. Yoshi took her _____ and nephew to the zoo.

8. I will need a ladder when I paint the _____.

9. The score of the baseball game was _____ to five.

10. The _____ news report lasted only thirty seconds.

11. A _____ thunderstorm blew over a tree in our yard.

12. The knight wore a suit of armor and carried a _____.

B Print the spelling word that fits in each shape.

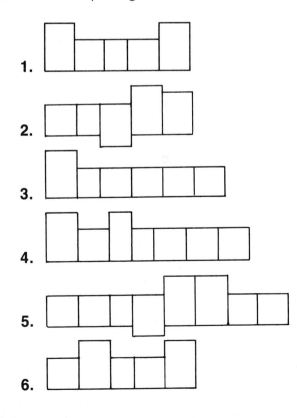

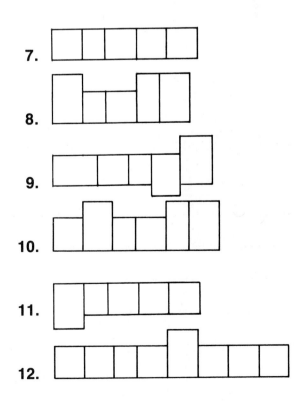

Dictionary

The words listed on a dictionary page are called **entry words.**
They are printed in dark letters to help you find them.

Entry words are divided into word parts called **syllables.**
A dot or space shows where a word is divided into syllables.

an·gry (ang′grē) *adj.* feeling or showing
anger. **an′ gri·er, an′ gri·est —an′gri·ly**
adv.

How many syllables
are in the word **angry**? _____

C Write the words below in alphabetical order. Look up each word in your
dictionary. Then write the word again, putting a dot between the syllables.

believe

reindeer

neighbor

ceiling

receive

cashier

1. _____   _____

2. _____   _____

3. _____   _____

4. _____   _____

5. _____   _____

6. _____   _____

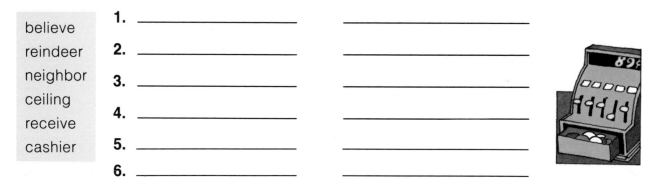

Build Word Power

Unscramble each group of letters to make the
spelling words that fit in the boxes.
Then use the letters in the numbered boxes
to fill in the blanks that answer the riddle.

1. c e e r i f
2. g l i n i c e
3. c e e n i
4. v e e r i c e
5. s h a c i r e
6. l e b e v i e
7. l e f i d
8. f e c h i
9. g i w e h
10. b o r e i g h n

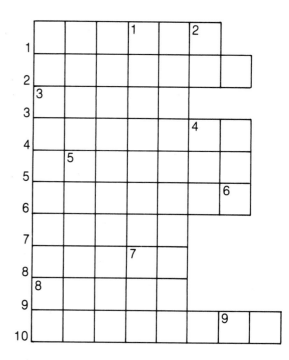

What kind of a bush does a kangaroo sit under when it rains?

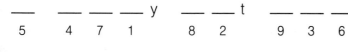
___ ___ ___ ___ y ___ ___ t ___ ___ ___
 5   4   7   1   8   2   9   3   6

chief	field	brief	receive	weigh
niece	fierce	believe	ceiling	neighbor
piece	shield	cashier	eight	reindeer

Reach Out for New Words

A You learned a rhyme on page 32 that helps you remember how to spell many **ie** and **ei** words. Write the new words that go with each part of the rhyme.

i before **e** _____   _____

_____   _____

except after **c** _____

or when sounded like **a** _____   _____

as in **neighbor** or **weigh** _____

Writing

B Write a new **ei** or **ie** word that has almost the same meaning as each word or phrase below.

1. bring back _____

2. ounces _____

3. sled _____

4. cargo _____

5. unexplored land _____

6. give way to _____

7. pain becoming less _____

8. too proud _____

Write one sentence using two of the new **ie** words. Write another sentence using two new **ei** words.

1. _____

_____

2. _____

_____

35

1
invite inviting
surprise surprising
promise promising

2
love lovely
complete completely
sincere sincerely

3
care careful
hope hopeful
sleeve sleeveless

4
speak
bread
break

5
coin
join
choice

6
they'll
doesn't
won't

7
believe
receive
neighbor

A An analogy is a special way of showing how words go together. Look at the first pair of words in each row. In what way do these words go together? Write a spelling word that makes the second pair of words go together in the same way as the first pair.

1. **love** is to **lovely** | as | **sincere** is to _____

2. **receive** is to **receiving** | as | **promise** is to _____

3. **would not** is to **wouldn't** | as | **does not** is to _____

4. **sincerely** is to **sincere** | as | **completely** is to _____

5. **believe** is to **believing** | as | **invite** is to _____

6. **careless** is to **careful** | as | **hopeless** is to _____

7. **you would** is to **you'd** | as | **will not** is to _____

8. **promising** is to **promise** | as | **surprising** is to _____

9. **hope** is to **hopeless** | as | **sleeve** is to _____

Proofreading

B Cross out each misspelled word. Write the correct spelling.

1. It is serprising that the vase didn't braek.

_____

2. We invited our nieghbor to have dinner with us.

_____

3. I'm hopefull that I'll recieve a good grade on that paper.

_____

4. Do you sincerly beleive what you just said?

_____

5. Craig may have the first choise.

_____

6. They'l be carefull not to touch the wet paint.

_____

C Write the word from the box that goes in each blank.

> bread believe coin receive speak neighbor
> break choice they'll lovely join completely

1. a ten cent _____
2. _____ the window
3. _____ finished
4. _____ the club
5. I think _____ agree
6. a slice of _____

7. our next door _____
8. _____ in ghosts
9. a _____ dress
10. _____ another language
11. _____ a letter
12. first _____

Using More Review Words

A Use the directions following each base word to make another form of the word.

1. **we**   form a contraction with **would** _____
2. **peace**   write the **ful** form _____
3. **there**   form a contraction with **is** _____
4. **tire**   write the **less** form _____
5. **slide**   write the **ing** form _____
6. **lone**   write the **ly** form _____
7. **serve**   write the **ing** form _____
8. **sure**   write the **ly** form _____
9. **fierce**   write the **ly** form _____
10. **you**   form a contraction with **would** _____
11. **wise**   write the **ly** form _____
12. **use**   write the **ful** form _____
13. **lose**   write the **ing** form _____
14. **shape**   write the **less** form _____

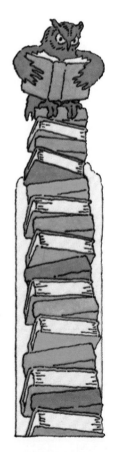

B Three words in each row follow the same spelling pattern. One word does not. Find that word. Be ready to tell why it does not belong.

1. boil   meat   soil   joint

   (**Meat** is the only word spelled with **ea**.)

2. cashier   reindeer   field   piece

3. hasn't   haven't   wouldn't   they're

4. nicely   bravely   scoring   closely

5. boiling   sharing   voting   shining

6. least   cream   meat   refuse

7. neighbor   eight   chief   weigh

8. spoiling   dreaming   sharing   pointing

9. here's   they'd   she's   there's

10. trading   wasteful   ageless   likely

C An analogy is a special way of showing how words go together. Look at the first pair of words in each row. In what way do these words go together? Write a word from the box that makes the second pair of words go together in the same way as the first pair.

ceiling	head	niece	bouncing	refusing
thread	fierce	eight	weigh	shining

1. **knit** is to **yarn**   as   **sew** is to   _____

2. **shoe** is to **foot**   as   **hat** is to   _____

3. **below** is to **floor**   as   **above** is to   _____

4. **yes** is to **accepting**   as   **no** is to   _____

5. **inches** are to **measure** as   **pounds** are to   _____

6. **lamb** is to **timid**   as   **lion** is to   _____

7. **star** is to **twinkling**   as   **sun** is to   _____

8. **four** is to **five**   as   **seven** is to   _____

9. **football** is to **kicking** as   **basketball** is to _____

10. **brother** is to **sister** as   **nephew** is to   _____

forward	breathing	soccer	bandaged
screaming	banner	skinned	soreness
bleachers	backward	goal	bleeding
shooting	court	wildly	moment
barely	toward	lying	limped

Prewriting. Prewriting is the thinking and planning you do before you begin to write. In this lesson, you will plan and write a **paragraph that tells what happened.**

Use Prewriting Skills

A Get ready to write about what happened at a sports event. You might choose a soccer game or basketball game, for example. Answer these questions with spelling words. The words will help you think of ideas for your paragraph.

1. What word names a sport? _____

2. What words tell the direction a player is moving?

_____   _____   _____

3. What **ed** action verbs could you use in your paragraph?

_____   _____   _____

4. What **ing** verbs might describe actions at a sports event?

_____   _____   _____

_____   _____

5. Where might the fans sit? _____ What might they

wave? _____

6. On what is a basketball game played? _____ What

does the player score? _____

7. What **ly** words could describe a player's actions?

_____   _____

B To plan a paragraph well, make notes about your topic. Write down your ideas. You will notice that many of your notes will tell about one particular idea. This can be the **main idea** of your paragraph.

Here are some prewriting notes Jody wrote about her first soccer game.

flat tire on the way	limped off the field
barely on time for the game	coach bandaged my leg
fell backward and skinned my knee	soccer is good exercise
my brother plays basketball	soreness lasted long after the game

Jody looked over her notes. Here's what she decided her main idea should be:

Everything went wrong the day I played my first soccer game.

Not all of Jody's notes fit that idea. Cross out those that do not belong. Then write the notes that do tell about Jody's main idea.

_____

_____

_____

_____

_____

_____

C The ideas in a paragraph must be in an order that makes sense. When you write a paragraph that tells a story, put the ideas in the order that they happened.

Look at the prewriting notes you wrote for Exercise B. Number them in an order that makes sense.

Now Think Plan your own paragraph about a sports event. Think about games you have seen or played. How did the fans act? What did the players do? Which moments were most exciting? You can make up your story or tell about something that really happened.

Follow these prewriting steps:

1. Choose your topic.
2. Make a list of ideas about your topic.
3. Read your notes to see how they fit together.
4. Decide on a main idea about your topic.
5. Cross out ideas that don't belong.
6. Number the rest in an order that makes sense.

Writing. Begin your paragraph with a topic sentence that tells the main idea. Write other sentences that tell about what happened. These sentences should add details about your main idea.

Use Writing Skills

Use good details to make your writing interesting. Expand each sentence by adding details to the simple subject and verb.

Example: Simple Subject → The <u>coach</u> | <u>shouted</u>. ← **Verb**

The excited soccer <u>coach</u> wildly <u>shouted</u> advice to the team captain.

1. <u>Fans</u> <u>were screaming</u>. _____

_____

2. The <u>soreness</u> <u>lasted</u>. _____

_____

3. The <u>bleachers</u> <u>were filled</u>. _____

_____

4. The <u>banner</u> <u>is hanging</u>. _____

_____

5. The <u>moment</u> <u>had arrived</u>. _____

_____

6. <u>Lauren</u> <u>limped</u>. _____

_____

7. <u>Doug</u> <u>was shooting</u>. _____

_____

Now Write Look at your prewriting notes. Use them to write a paragraph about a sports event. Begin with a strong topic sentence that tells what the paragraph is about. Tell things in the order that they happened. Try to write interesting sentences that have good details.

Revising and Proofreading. Your writing is not finished until you have revised your paragraph. When you revise, you make changes to improve your writing. First revise your ideas. Change words or sentences to make them better. Then proofread carefully to find mistakes in capitalization, punctuation, and spelling.

One important part of revising is checking to see that you have chosen lively language. In a paragraph that tells what happened, you want to use verbs that show vivid action.

> **Example:** Chris <u>went</u> to first base. (weak verb)
> Chris <u>raced</u> to first base. (strong verb)

Use Revising and Proofreading Skills

A Rewrite the following sentences. Replace the underlined words with spelling words. The spelling words should be verbs that show vivid action.

1. The fans were <u>making noise</u> in the stands.

_____

2. One player was <u>throwing</u> the ball at the basket.

_____

3. Suddenly she tripped and <u>hurt</u> her knee.

_____

4. The injured player <u>walked</u> off the court.

_____

B Proofread this first part of a paragraph about a baseball game. Mark all mistakes in capitalization, punctuation, and spelling. Then rewrite the paragraph correctly on your own paper.

Remember
- Begin every sentence with a capital letter.
- Indent the first line of a paragraph.
- End every sentence with the correct end mark.

My gaol in baseball was to reach first base. the coach sent me to bat in

every game I struck out wildly every time At last my momeant came? I was

breething hard as I waited for the pitch. Would I finally get my single.

43

C Revise the following paragraph. Then rewrite it correctly on your own paper. The directions below will help you.

1. Cross out one sentence that is not about the main idea.
2. Underline one sentence that is out of order. Draw an arrow to show where it should go.
3. Replace the two underlined verbs with stronger verbs from your spelling list.
4. Cross out the six misspelled words. Write them correctly on the lines.
5. Correct the capitalization errors in lines 3 and 8.
6. Correct one punctuation error in line 4.

1   Wilson Clark was the hero of the Hilltop basketball team yesterday.

2 Hilltop had won by two points!   The score was tied a moment before the

3 game ended.   A forwerd quickly passed the ball to wilson.   He raced all

4 the way down the cort and suddenly fell backward   He landed on his

5 back, but he was still holding the ball.   He knew he didn't have time to get

6 up and continue running.   There wasn't even time to pass the ball to

7 another player.   Wilson realized that there was only one thing to do.

8 Lyeng on the floor, he tried <u>throwing</u> a basket.   he scord the goal as the

9 buzzer ended the game.   Fans in the bleechers began <u>calling</u> wildley the

10 minute the buzzer sounded.   Wilson gets good grades too.

_____   _____   _____

_____   _____   _____

Now Revise   Read your own sports story. Does each sentence tell about the main idea? Are your sentences in an order that makes sense? Have you used the best words? Remember to proofread for mistakes in capitalization, punctuation, and spelling. Copy the paragraph in your best handwriting.

Now you've written a paragraph you should be proud of. Share your paragraph with other students. Show them how you are learning the process of writing.

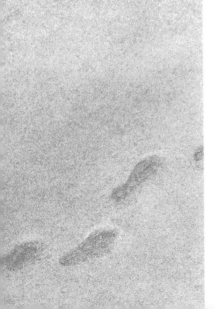

A Writer's Journal

Reading poetry can give you ideas for writing in your journal. A poem may talk about feelings or experiences you have had. A poem may also help you see ordinary things in fresh, new ways.

Read the poem and think about what it means. Then discuss the questions with the class.

1. Who is Hanna? How does the speaker feel about Hanna?

2. What does the speaker mean by lines such as "Chocolate ice cream tastes like prunes" or "Velvet feels like hay"? What do these things have to do with a friend moving away?

Now use the poem as a starting point for your next journal entry. Here are some ideas you might want to use:

1. Write about a friend who moved away. Describe how you felt.

2. The speaker in the poem describes her feelings by telling us that many good things no longer seem good. Write about an experience that made you sad or angry. You may want to describe your feelings the way the speaker in the poem describes hers. Use the following as sentence ideas:

_____ tasted like _____.
_____ smelled like _____.

SINCE HANNA MOVED AWAY

The tires on my bike are flat.
The sky is grouchy gray.
At least it sure feels like that
Since Hanna moved away.

Chocolate ice cream tastes
    like prunes.
December's come to stay.
They've taken back the Mays
    and Junes
Since Hanna moved away.

Flowers smell like halibut.
Velvet feels like hay.
Every handsome dog's a mutt
Since Hanna moved away.

Nothing's fun to laugh about.
Nothing's fun to play.
They call me, but I won't
    come out
Since Hanna moved away.

—JUDITH VIORST

Building a Personal Word List

If you do not know how to spell a word, follow these steps.

1. Write the word as you think it should be spelled.

2. After writing, see if the word is on your personal word list. If not, look up the word in the dictionary.

3. Correct your spelling. Add the word to your personal word list.

4. Practice spelling the word several times.

holiday	holidays
highway	highways
chimney	chimneys
jockey	jockeys
journey	journeys
subway	subways
display	displays
story	stories
country	countries
family	families
canary	canaries
duty	duties
library	libraries
blueberry	blueberries
flurry	flurries

A word that names something is called a **noun**.
A noun that names *one* thing is a **singular** noun.
A noun that names *more than one* thing is a **plural** noun.

1. The words in the first column are singular. How many end with **vowel + y**? _____

   How many end with **consonant + y**? _____

2. The words in the second column are plural.

   What is the last letter of the **vowel + y** words? ____

   What are the last three letters of the **consonant + y** words? _____

To make the plural form of a noun that ends with **vowel + y**,
   add the letter **s**.
To make the plural form of a noun that ends with **consonant + y**,
   change the **y** to **i** and add **es**.

Practice the Words

A Print the spelling word that fits in each shape.

1. [word shape grid]
2. [word shape grid]
3. [word shape grid]
4. [word shape grid]
5. [word shape grid]
6. [word shape grid]
7. [word shape grid]
8. [word shape grid]
9. [word shape grid]
10. [word shape grid]
11. [word shape grid]
12. [word shape grid]

B Write the seven base words that go in the blanks. Then write the plural form of each word.

Last fall, my __1__ decided to spend the Labor Day __2__ in the __3__. As we drove down the __4__, we each took turns telling a __5__, and then we all sang songs. After a time, we drove through a beautiful valley. It was filled with apple trees, __6__ bushes, and fields of vegetables. There was only one house in the valley. It was very large and had a tall __7__. My little brother wondered if a green giant lived there.

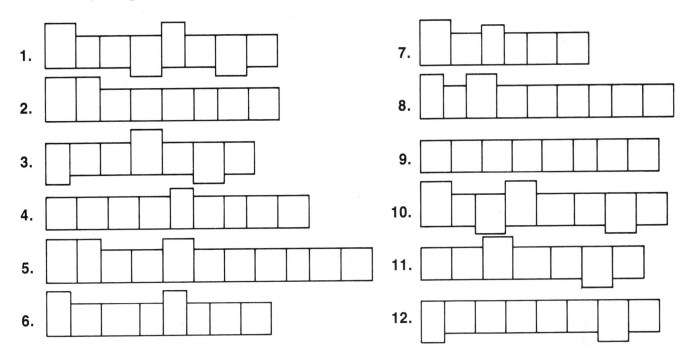

	Singular	Plural
1.	_____	_____
2.	_____	_____
3.	_____	_____
4.	_____	_____
5.	_____	_____
6.	_____	_____
7.	_____	_____

C Use the clues to find the spelling words that fit in the puzzle.

Across

2. yellow birds
5. special days
6. jobs
10. underground trains
11. places where books are kept
12. people who ride horses

Down

1. brothers, sisters, and parents
3. fairy tales
4. smoke goes up these
7. trips
8. shows
9. a few snowflakes

Build Word Power

Each word below is part of a plural spelling word. Write the spelling word. Use each word only once.

1. key _____
2. can _____
3. high _____
4. lid _____
5. am _____
6. ties _____

7. our _____
8. him _____
9. or _____
10. tries _____
11. is _____
12. blue _____

holidays   jockeys   displays   families   libraries
highways   journeys   stories   canaries   blueberries
chimneys   subways   countries duties   flurries

Discover new words below!

Reach Out for New Words

A Use the code to find seven new words that are described by the sentences. Each number stands for one letter of the alphabet. Print the correct letter in the blank above each number.

j	q	f	m	a	i	s	c	g	r	x	b	z	h	u	p	d	k	o	y	t	e	l	w	v	n
1	2	3	4	5	6	7	8	9	10	11	12	13	14	15	16	17	18	19	20	21	22	23	24	25	26

1. Football players wear them.

   ___ ___ ___ ___ ___ ___ ___
   1   22 10 7   22 20 7

2. Machines are used to make things here.

   ___ ___ ___ ___ ___ ___ ___ ___ ___
   3   5   8   21 19 10 6   22 7

3. You shop for these in the supermarket.

   ___ ___ ___ ___ ___ ___ ___ ___ ___
   9   10 19 8   22 10 6   22 7

4. They make a flashlight shine.

   ___ ___ ___ ___ ___ ___ ___ ___ ___
   12 5   21 21 22 10 6   22 7

5. Winners often receive them.

   ___ ___ ___ ___ ___ ___ ___ ___
   21 10 19 16 14 6   22 7

6. Trains run on them.

   ___ ___ ___ ___ ___ ___ ___ ___
   10 5   6   23 24 5   20 7

7. Pads and helmets protect athletes from them.

   ___ ___ ___ ___ ___ ___ ___ ___
   6   26 1   15 10 6   22 7

Dictionary

B Write the new words in alphabetical order. Then write the base form of each word. Look up each base word in your spelling dictionary. Write the base word again, putting dots between the syllables.

Spelling Words	Base Words	Syllables
1. _____	_____	_____
2. _____	_____	_____
3. _____	_____	_____
4. _____	_____	_____
5. _____	_____	_____
6. _____	_____	_____
7. _____	_____	_____

tiny	tinier	tiniest
busy	busier	busiest
early	earlier	earliest
icy	icier	iciest
curly	curlier	curliest
angry	angrier	angriest
friendly	friendlier	friendliest
silly	sillier	silliest

A word that describes a noun is called an **adjective**.

1. What is the last letter of each word in the first column? ___

2. Is the letter before the **y** a vowel or a consonant? _____

3. What are the last two letters of the words in the second column? _____

4. What are the last three letters of the words in the third column? _____

5. When **er** and **est** were added to the words in the

first column, the final **y** was changed to what letter? ___

The ending **er** can be added to make an adjective mean *more*.
    Spot is <u>tinier</u> than Pepper.

The ending **est** can be added to make an adjective mean *most*.
    Spot is the <u>tiniest</u> of the three dogs.

When an adjective ends with **consonant + y**, change the **y** to **i**
    before you add **er** or **est**.

A Write the form of the spelling word in parentheses that goes in each blank. Use the **er** form when you compare two people or things. Use the **est** form when you compare three or more people or things.

1. The sidewalk is _____ than the driveway. (icy)

2. Tom is the _____ boy in our class. (friendly)

3. The sun sets _____ in the winter than in summer. (early)

4. That joke is even _____ than the one Janet told. (silly)

5. The _____ puppy in the litter is the one I want. (tiny)

6. On what day of the year is the _____ sunrise? (early)

7. My sister has the _____ hair in our family. (curly)

8. The _____ clown in the circus wears a bright orange wig. (silly)

9. Monday is the _____ day of the week for me. (busy)

10. That newborn hamster is _____ than a quarter. (tiny)

11. A poodle has _____ hair than a collie. (curly)

12. The fans were _____ than the losing team. (angry)

B Find the misspelled word in each group. Write the word correctly.

1. erlier
curly
busiest
tiniest

_____

2. curlier
friendlyer
busy
earliest

_____

3. friendliest
curly
silliest
angryest

_____

4. early
angry
sillier
curlliest

_____

5. tinier
silly
busyer
icy

_____

6. friendly
angrier
tiny
iceyest

_____

C Unscramble the **er** form of each spelling word and write it. Then write the **est** form.

1. larriee　　　_____　　　_____

2. brusie　　　_____　　　_____

3. riniet　　　_____　　　_____

4. slirile　　　_____　　　_____

5. rangeir　　　_____　　　_____

6. drieflienr　　　_____　　　_____

7. ricie　　　_____　　　_____

8. licreur　　　_____　　　_____

Build Word Power

Writing

Each sentence below gives you some information. Write a question you might ask to find out more information. Use the **er** or **est** form of a spelling word in your question.

1. Betty and Meg have <u>curly</u> hair.

Whose hair is curlier? _____

2. All the students in our class are <u>friendly</u>.

_____

3. The clowns in this circus are <u>silly</u>.

_____

4. Barb and Suzanne have <u>tiny</u> dogs.

_____

5. Monday and Tuesday will be very <u>busy</u> days.

_____

tinier	busiest	icier	curliest	friendlier	silliest
tiniest	earlier	iciest	angrier	friendliest	
busier	earliest	curlier	angriest	sillier	

New Words

merry	dizzy
fancy	hazy
greedy	juicy
ugly	

Reach Out for New Words

A Write the **er** and **est** forms of each new word.

1. _____ _____

2. _____ _____

3. _____ _____

4. _____ _____

5. _____ _____

6. _____ _____

7. _____ _____

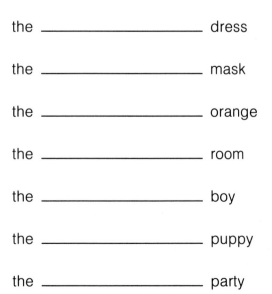

B Write the **est** form of the new word that describes each person or thing below.

1. the dress with the most
   lace and ribbons on it   the _____ dress

2. the mask with green skin,
   bloodshot eyes, and a wart   the _____ mask

3. the orange with the most
   liquid inside it   the _____ orange

4. the room with the most dust
   and smoke in it   the _____ room

5. the boy who turned the most
   cartwheels   the _____ boy

6. the puppy who ate the whole
   box of dog biscuits   the _____ puppy

7. the party at which everyone
   had a wonderful time   the _____ party

try	trying	tried
deny	denying	denied
reply	replying	replied
bury	burying	buried
study	studying	studied
worry	worrying	worried
empty	emptying	emptied
multiply	multiplying	multiplied

A **verb** is a word that tells about an action.
A verb that tells about an action that happened in the past is in the **past tense**.

1. The words in the first column can all be verbs.
   Is the letter before each final **y** a consonant or a vowel? _____

2. What three letters were added to make the words in the second column? _____

3. Did the **y** change before **ing** was added? _____

4. The words in the last column are in the past
   tense. What are the last two letters of these words? _____

5. What happened to the **y** when the **ed** was added? _____

When an ending is added to a verb that ends with **consonant + y**,
change the **y** to **i** unless the ending is **ing**.

A Complete each sentence with the **ed** or **ing** form of a spelling word.

1. The pirate _____ the treasure near a large rock.

2. Kay didn't sleep because she was _____ about her grades.

3. Lou is _____ the wastebaskets.

4. I was still _____ when the math test ended.

5. The swimmer _____ to beat the school record.

6. Pat is _____ to the letter from his pen pal.

7. Alex is _____ for the history test.

8. Mom _____ the carton of milk into the pitcher.

9. I got the right answer when I _____ the two numbers.

10. Tom is _____ to fix the chain on his bike.

11. Chris _____ correctly to the teacher's question.

12. Ben _____ hard for the science test.

13. Our dog is _____ his bone in the backyard.

14. Barry _____ having started the rumor.

15. The farmer _____ about the crops when it got cold.

B Look at each word. If it is spelled correctly, draw a 😊 . If it is misspelled, write the word correctly.

1. bureying _____	7. empteing _____
2. spying _____	8. worying _____
3. marrying _____	9. crying _____
4. repliing _____	10. denyed _____
5. multiplyed _____	11. copied _____
6. tryed _____	12. studyed _____

Dictionary

A dictionary **entry** is made up of an **entry word** and all the information that follows it.

Many entry words are base words. Words with endings, or **word forms**, are often included in the entries for base words.

try (trī) *v.* to make an effort. —**tried, try′ ing**	For example, the word forms **tried** and **trying** are included in the entry for **try**.

C What entry word would you look up to find each word?

1. trying   _____

2. multiplying   _____

3. replied   _____

4. worried   _____

5. buried   _____

6. emptied   _____

7. studying   _____

8. denying   _____

Build Word Power

Writing

Write a sentence to answer each question. Use the past tense of the underlined word.

1. How long did you <u>study</u> last night?

_____

2. What numbers did you <u>multiply</u>?

_____

3. Where did the dog <u>bury</u> the bone?

_____

4. What did you <u>try</u> to make?

_____

5. What did the coach <u>worry</u> about?

_____

6. What did he <u>deny</u> having done?

_____

trying	denied	burying	studied	emptying	multiplied
tried	replying	buried	worrying	emptied	
denying	replied	studying	worried	multiplying	

New Words

magnify
pity
occupy
supply
steady
satisfy

Reach Out for New Words

A Write the **ing** form and the past tense of each new word.

1. _____   _____

2. _____   _____

3. _____   _____

4. _____   _____

5. _____   _____

6. _____   _____

B Use each clue to find a new word that fits in the puzzle. Each word will end with **ed** or **ing.**

Across
4. providing things
5. kept from moving
6. made something look larger

Down
1. feeling sorry for
2. living in
3. pleased

paw   drawing
law   crawling
claw   yawned
straw   thawed
lawn   sawdust
dawn   outlaw
shawl   coleslaw
           strawberry

Look at the first seven words.

1. What two letters do you see in every word? _____

2. How many syllables are in each word? _____

3. In how many words does **aw** come at the end? _____

4. In how many words is **aw** followed by **n**? _____

5. In how many words is **aw** followed by **l**? _____

Look at the next eight words.

6. How many words have the ending **ing**? _____ **ed**? _____

The letters **aw** are found in many one-syllable words.
They may come at the end of the word or just before **l** or **n** .

Practice the Words

A Use each clue to find a spelling word that fits in the boxes. The letter **a** has been given to help you.

1. a dog's foot
2. short grass around a house
3. when the sun comes up
4. opened your mouth sleepily
5. wood dust left after sawing
6. a sharp nail on an animal's foot
7. clothing that wraps around the shoulders
8. became unfrozen
9. making a picture
10. moving on hands and knees
11. a tube for drinking
12. a red fruit
13. someone who breaks laws
14. a cabbage salad

Words that have almost the same meaning are called **synonyms.**

B Write the spelling word that is the synonym of each word below.

1. melted _____
2. rule _____
3. sunrise _____
4. sketching _____
5. foot _____
6. nail _____
7. hay _____
8. creeping _____

C Unscramble each group of letters to make a spelling word.

1. nawl _____
2. clingwar _____
3. wap _____
4. warst _____
5. awl _____
6. wringad _____
7. dawney _____
8. whated _____

9. tusswad _____
10. twalou _____
11. lawc _____
12. brewstarry _____
13. washl _____
14. dwan _____
15. scloawle _____

Build Word Power

Write the spelling word that goes with each word group.

1. orange, cherry, apple, _____
2. hopping, creeping, walking, _____
3. painting, sketching, coloring, _____
4. cape, sweater, jacket, _____
5. afternoon, evening, noon, _____
6. foot, hoof, hand, _____
7. French fries, baked beans, potato salad, _____
8. whistled, chewed, talked, _____

paw	straw	shawl	yawned	outlaw
law	lawn	drawing	thawed	coleslaw
claw	dawn	crawling	sawdust	strawberry

New Words

flaw	lawyer
fawn	bawling
awning	scrawled
sprawled	rawhide
scrawny	

Reach Out for New Words

A Words are printed in three directions in this puzzle. → ↓ ↘ Find the nine new **aw** words. Circle each word and write it.

```
j r h f l a w s d
k p a a c b g p f
q l a w y e r r b
s m n n h l r a a
x c w v t i s w w
v d r c b f d l l
k g p a d z v e i
s c r a w l e d n
h t l a w n i n g
n m s c b q y w j
```

1. _____
2. _____
3. _____
4. _____
5. _____
6. _____
7. _____
8. _____
9. _____

Writing

B Write four sentences using two or more **aw** words in each sentence. Use all your new **aw** words. You may also use list words. Circle the **aw** words in each sentence.

1. *I yawned when I woke at dawn to mow the lawn.*

2. _____

_____

3. _____

_____

4. _____

_____

5. _____

_____

fault
haunt
launch
laundry
faucet
August
author
autumn
sauce
saucer
because
applaud
caught
taught
daughter

1. What two letters do you see in every word? _____

2. Do these letters come at the end of the word? _____

The letters **au** are usually found at the beginning
or in the middle of a word.

Practice the Words

A Use each clue to find a spelling word that fits in the puzzle.

Across

3. gravy
6. to clap hands
7. to set off a rocket
8. a dish under a cup
11. helped someone learn
13. a female child
14. what a ghost does

Down

1. for this reason
2. blame
4. the month after July
5. what water comes through
7. clothes to be washed
9. a writer
10. captured
12. the season after summer

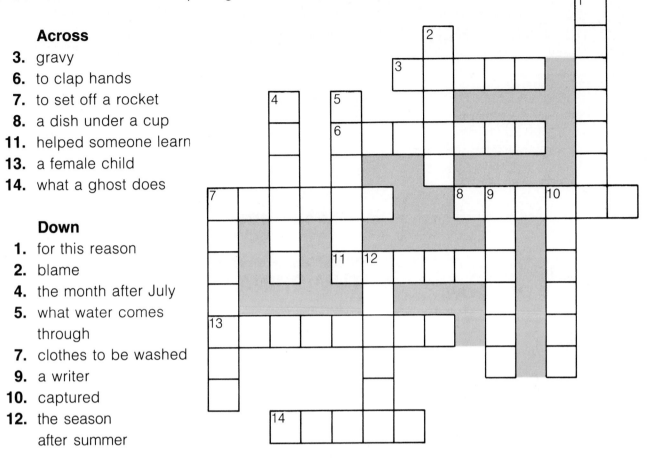

B Answer each question with spelling words.

1. Which three words begin with the letters **au**?

   _____   _____   _____

2. Which three words have the letters **augh**?

   _____   _____   _____

3. Which three words have the letters **aun**?

   _____   _____   _____

4. Which three words have the letters **auce**?

   _____   _____   _____

Proofreading

C Find the eight misspelled words in the newspaper advertisements and headlines below. Write each word correctly.

Critics Aplaud Play by Local Auther

SQUEAKY CLEANERS

- Complete lawndry service available
- We remove all stains, from grass to spaghetti sauce

576 Main Street

Leaky faucet?
Call Pete the Plumber!
555-8247

Rain at Fawlt in Delayed Rocket Launch

Schools Close Becuse of Snow

Millers' Department Store
AUTUM CHINA SALE!
Buy a dinner plate, cup and sauser for $15!
Service for 8 only $110!
No payments until Augist!

1. _____
2. _____
3. _____
4. _____
5. _____
6. _____
7. _____
8. _____

Build Word Power

One word will sometimes make you think of another word. For example, the word **paw** may make you think of a dog because a dog's foot is called a paw.

Each underlined word below goes with one of your spelling words. Write the spelling word. Then write a sentence using both words.

1. Ghost goes with _____.

_____

2. Cup goes with _____.

_____

3. Story goes with _____.

_____

4. Ball goes with _____.

_____

5. Water goes with _____.

_____

fault	laundry	author	saucer	caught
haunt	faucet	autumn	because	taught
launch	August	sauce	applaud	daughter

New Words
Discover new words below!

Reach Out for New Words

A Find eight new **au** words by following this code. Each letter in a word goes with a capital letter and a number. For example: B2 = h.

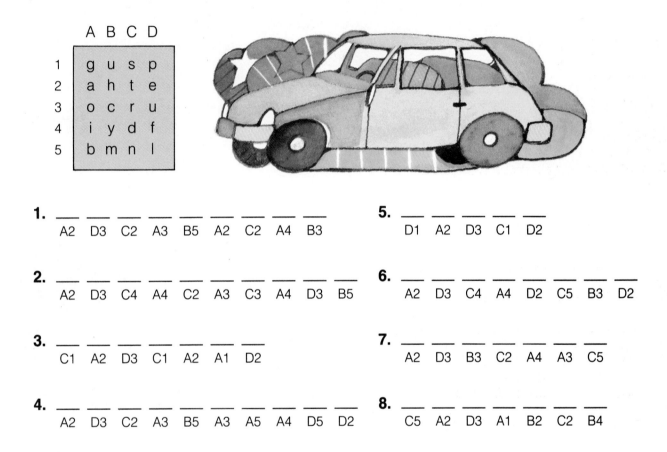

	A	B	C	D
1	g	u	s	p
2	a	h	t	e
3	o	c	r	u
4	i	y	d	f
5	b	m	n	l

1. __ __ __ __ __ __ __ __ __
   A2 D3 C2 A3 B5 A2 C2 A4 B3

5. __ __ __ __ __
   D1 A2 D3 C1 D2

2. __ __ __ __ __ __ __ __ __ __
   A2 D3 C4 A4 C2 A3 C3 A4 D3 B5

6. __ __ __ __ __ __ __ __
   A2 D3 C4 A4 D2 C5 B3 D2

3. __ __ __ __ __ __ __
   C1 A2 D3 C1 A2 A1 D2

7. __ __ __ __ __ __ __
   A2 D3 B3 C2 A4 A3 C5

4. __ __ __ __ __ __ __ __ __ __
   A2 D3 C2 A3 B5 A3 A5 A4 D5 D2

8. __ __ __ __ __ __ __
   C5 A2 D3 A1 B2 C2 B4

B Add the missing vowels to complete each word. Then match each word with its meaning.

1. __ __ d __ __ nc __   behaving badly

2. p __ __ s __   a special kind of sale

3. n __ __ ghty   a kind of breakfast meat

4. __ __ t __ m __ b __ l __   people seeing a play or concert

5. __ __ d __ t __ r __ __ m   a short stop

6. __ __ ct __ __ n   keeps working by itself

7. __ __ t __ m __ t __ c   a car

8. s __ __ s __ g __   a large room for performances

65

shout
proud
sour
blouse
ounce
pound
thousand
amount

eyebrow
clown
drown
howl
growl
flower
power

1. In how many words do you see the letters **ou**? _____

2. Does **ou** ever come at the end of a word? _____

   at the beginning? _____ in the middle? _____

3. In how many words do you see the letters **ow**? _____

4. Does **ow** ever come at the end of a word? _____

5. What letter or letters come after **ow** in **clown** and **drown**? _____

   in **howl** and **growl**? _____ in **flower** and **power**? _____

Sometimes it is difficult to decide whether to spell a word with the letters **ou** or **ow.**

The letters **ou** are usually found at the beginning or in the middle of a word.

The letters **ow** are usually found at the end of a word or followed by one **n,** one **l,** or the letters **er.**

Practice the Words

A Use each clue to find a spelling word that fits in the boxes.

1. yell

2. the cry of a wolf

3. snarl

4. a shirt

5. opposite of **sweet**

6. how much

7. sixteen of these make a pound

8. pleased with yourself

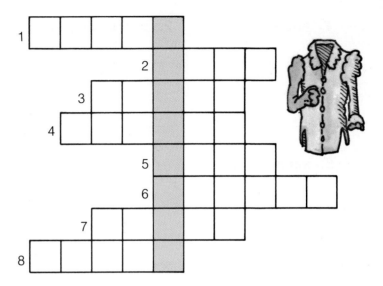

Write the word that is hidden in the colored boxes. _____

9. a measure of weight

10. hair above the eye

11. a rose

12. strength

13. a funny person

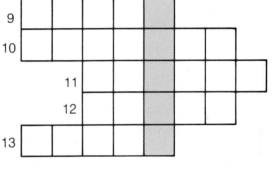

Write the word that is hidden in the colored boxes. _____

B Look at each word. If it is spelled correctly, draw a ☺. If it is misspelled, write the word correctly.

1. sour _____

2. power _____

3. thousend _____

4. showt _____

5. proud _____

6. growel _____

7. flower _____

8. amownt _____

9. drown _____

10. cloun _____

11. bloues _____

12. ownse _____

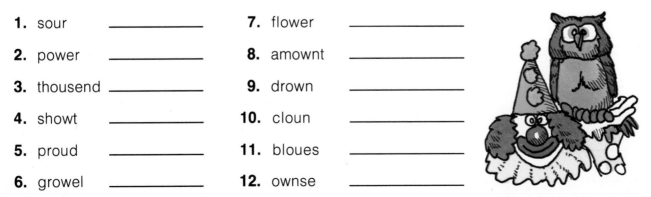

Dictionary

C The words below are dictionary guide words. What spelling words would appear on the same page as each pair of guide words? Write them in alphabetical order.

1. shore/town

_____

_____

_____

2. cheese/eyelash

_____

_____

_____

3. flat/huddle

_____

_____

_____

4. other/puddle

_____

_____

_____

_____

5. among/cabin

_____

_____

Build Word Power

Writing

Choose a spelling word and write an acrostic poem about your word. Let the spelling word be the *title* of the poem. Begin each line with a letter of the spelling word.

Growl
Grumbling and
rumbling, the
old lion
was guarding his
lair.

_____

_____

_____

_____

_____

shout	blouse	thousand	clown	growl
proud	ounce	amount	drown	flower
sour	pound	eyebrow	howl	power

Reach Out for New Words

A Write the new **ou** or **ow** word that matches each meaning.
Then circle the **ou** or **ow** in each word.

1. to let _____

2. to be on all sides _____

3. start to grow _____

4. a long table top _____

5. to sneak _____

6. a tall, narrow building _____

7. a sofa _____

Writing

B Read each pair of sentences. Put the two sentences together to make one
sentence that includes the underlined word.

1. Maple trees <u>surround</u> the house. Oak trees <u>surround</u> the house.

_____

2. The <u>couch</u> is soft. The <u>couch</u> is comfortable.

_____

3. Lions <u>prowl</u> in the jungle. Tigers <u>prowl</u> in the jungle.

_____

4. I can see over the <u>counter</u>. The <u>counter</u> is in the office.

_____

5. Tulips <u>sprout</u> in the spring. Daffodils <u>sprout</u> in the spring.

_____

Words spelled with ough or ould

through

cough

bought

brought

thought

fought

dough

though

rough

enough

could

would

should

shoulder

boulder

1. What two letters do you see in every word? _____

2. What group of four letters do you see in ten of the words? _____

3. In how many words do the letters **ough** sound like **oo** in the word **too**? _____

   like **aw** in **paw**? _____   like **o** in **go**? _____   like **uff** in **cuff**? _____

4. What group of four letters do you see in five of the words? _____

Many words are spelled with the letter group **ough**.
This letter group can be pronounced in several different ways.
A few words are spelled with the letter group **ould**.

Practice the Words

A Write the spelling words that complete these sentences.

1. Tim went shopping and _____ some new socks.

2. _____ you like to come to my house for dinner?

3. Carol _____ some games to our party.

4. I _____ I heard the door creak open!

5. Jim tried, but he _____ not lift that heavy box.

6. Pete is making _____ for our pizza.

7. The two dogs _____ for the meaty bone.

8. Robin went swimming even _____ the water was cold.

9. You _____ wear knee pads when you skate.

10. Do we have _____ wood to build a clubhouse?

11. This gravel road is very _____.

12. The train track runs _____ a tunnel in the mountain.

13. Football players wear helmets and _____ pads.

14. Smoke from the campfire made Ellen _____.

15. Sam sat on a huge _____ at the edge of the river.

B Add the missing letters to complete each word. Then write the word.

1. e __ o __ g __   _____

2. b __ u __ h __   _____

3. b __ u __ d __ r   _____

4. t __ r __ u __ h   _____

5. t __ o __ g __ t   _____

6. d __ u __ h   _____

7. s __ o __ l __ e __   _____

8. c __ u __ h   _____

9. c __ u __ d   _____

71

C Write the two words that rhyme with each clue word and fit in the shapes.

1. caught

_____   _____

2. good

_____   _____

3. blow

_____   _____

4. stuff

_____   _____

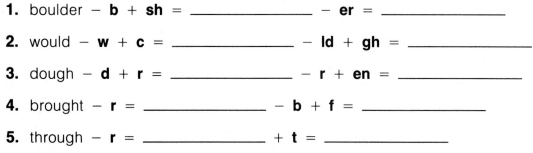

Build Word Power

Follow the **+** and **−** signs to change each spelling word into another spelling word. All your spelling words are included in this exercise.

1. boulder **− b + sh** = _____ **− er** = _____

2. would **− w + c** = _____ **− ld + gh** = _____

3. dough **− d + r** = _____ **− r + en** = _____

4. brought **− r** = _____ **− b + f** = _____

5. through **− r** = _____ **+ t** = _____

through	brought	dough	enough	should
cough	thought	though	could	shoulder
bought	fought	rough	would	boulder

New Words
Discover new words below!

Reach Out for New Words

A Fifteen **ough** words are in this poem. Write the six new **ough** words that are not on your spelling list. Not all of the new words will be in heavy type.

I take it you already know
about **tough** and **rough**
And **cough** and **dough**,

And if you tried I know you could
Remember words
Like **would** and **should**.

Now if you don't, you really ought
To learn **although**
and **thought** and **fought**.

And so your list will really grow
Learn **trough** and **bought**
Thorough and **though.**

And if that's not enough for you
Then think of words
Like **sought** and **through**.

A silly language? I agree
How did we speak it
At the age of three?

I'm sure you know before I tell it
The problem now
Is how to spell it!

1. _____

2. _____

3. _____

4. _____

5. _____

6. _____

B Use each riddle to find one of your new **ough** words.

1. where horses drink; shaped like  _____

2. the antonym of **weak**; rhymes with **stuff** _____

3. has five letters; used instead of **should** _____

4. means the same as **looked for**; shaped like ⬚⬚⬚⬚⬚ _____

5. synonym for **but**; has two syllables _____

6. means **complete**; rhymes with **burrow** _____

73

10
holiday   holidays
chimney   chimneys
family   families

11
tiny   tinier   tiniest
busy   busier   busiest
friendly   friendlier   friendliest

12
try   trying   tried
reply   replying   replied
bury   burying   buried

13
drawing
lawn
crawling

14
autumn
because
taught

15
amount
growl
flower

16
thought
enough
would

A An analogy is a special way of showing how words go together. Look at the first pair of words in each row. In what way do these words go together? Write a spelling word that makes the second pair of words go together in the same way as the first pair.

1. **easy** is to **easier**   as   **tiny** is to   _____

2. **try** is to **trying**   as   **reply** is to   _____

3. **holiday** is to **holidays**   as   **chimney** is to   _____

4. **try** is to **tried**   as   **bury** is to   _____

5. **tiniest** is to **tiny**   as   **busiest** is to   _____

6. **reply** is to **replies**   as   **family** is to   _____

7. **tinier** is to **tiniest**   as   **busier** is to   _____

8. **replied** is to **replying**   as   **tried** is to   _____

Proofreading

B Cross out each misspelled word. Write the word correctly.

1. A small amownt of glue will be enuf.

   _____

2. I thougt Bill's house woud be easy to find.

   _____

3. Last year our familys spent the holidais together.

   _____

4. That building has two chimnies.

   _____

5. The baby is crauling, but he's not walking yet.

   _____

6. I like autum becaus of the cool weather.

   _____

C Complete each phrase with a word from the box.

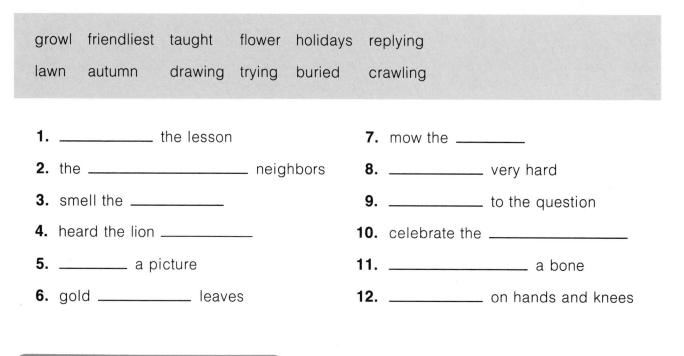

growl	friendliest	taught	flower	holidays	replying
lawn	autumn	drawing	trying	buried	crawling

1. _____ the lesson

2. the _____ neighbors

3. smell the _____

4. heard the lion _____

5. _____ a picture

6. gold _____ leaves

7. mow the _____

8. _____ very hard

9. _____ to the question

10. celebrate the _____

11. _____ a bone

12. _____ on hands and knees

Using More Review Words

A Use the directions following each base word to make another form of the word.

1. **icy**   write the **est** form   _____

2. **deny**   write the past tense   _____

3. **study**   write the **ing** form   _____

4. **silly**   write the **est** form   _____

5. **library**   write the plural   _____

6. **multiply**   write the past tense   _____

7. **early**   write the **er** form   _____

8. **country**   write the plural   _____

9. **blueberry**   write the plural   _____

10. **worry**   write the **ing** form   _____

11. **empty**   write the past tense   _____

12. **highway**   write the plural   _____

13. **angry**   write the **est** form   _____

14. **curly**   write the **er** form   _____

15. **canary**   write the plural   _____

B Three words in each row follow the same spelling pattern. One word does not. Find that word. Be ready to tell why it does not belong.

1. paw   claw   howl   straw

2. caught   brought   taught   daughter

3. dawn   shawl   law   clown

4. angrier   earliest   busier   icier

5. proud   should   would   could

6. duties   stories   countries   jockeys

7. sour   power   blouse   shout

8. haunt   launch   applaud   coleslaw

9. flurries   journeys   subways   displays

10. blouse   saucer   faucet   fault

C Complete these analogies. Write a word from the box that makes the second pair of words go together in the same way as the first pair.

author	rough	dawn	August	daughter
shawl	shoulder	boulder	claw	dough

1. **boy** is to **son**   as   **girl** is to   _____

2. **person** is to **fingernail**   as   **animal** is to   _____

3. **leg** is to **hip**   as   **arm** is to   _____

4. **painting** is to **artist**   as   **book** is to   _____

5. **January** is to **February**   as   **July** is to   _____

6. **cake** is to **batter**   as   **bread** is to   _____

7. **small** is to **large**   as   **pebble** is to   _____

8. **silk** is to **smooth**   as   **sandpaper** is to   _____

9. **head** is to **scarf**   as   **shoulders** are to   _____

10. **evening** is to **sunset**   as   **morning** is to   _____

cabin	dust	gloomy	rusty
rented	iron	scent	wooden
spooky	lamp	stairs	steep
curtains	mist	hinge	stove
damp	pine	lantern	bucket

Prewriting. Prewriting is the thinking and planning you do before you begin to write. In this lesson, you will plan and write a **description.** You will imagine or remember a scene. Then you will use sense details to share the sight and feeling with others.

Use Prewriting Skills

A Answer the questions with spelling words. The words will help you think of ways to describe an old house.

1. What kind of tree might you see outside the house? _____

2. What words make you think of wetness in the air?

   _____   _____

3. What words might describe the stairs?

   _____   _____

4. What words might describe an old door hinge?

   _____   _____

5. What words could describe the way the house feels to you?

   _____   _____

6. What might everything inside an old deserted house be covered with? _____

7. What specific household items might you see inside the house?

   _____   _____   _____

   _____   _____

8. What type of house could it be? _____

B Before you write, decide what feeling you want your description to have. The feeling might be happy, sad, scary, peaceful, or exciting. Choose your words to give this feeling.

Write the phrase from each pair that you would choose to create a scary feeling in your description.

1. rented a spooky cabin
   rented a log cabin

   _____

2. gloomy clouds
   bright sunshine

   _____

3. heavy, dark curtains
   clean, white curtains

   _____

4. smoky iron stove
   warm kitchen stove

   _____

5. sweet pine scent
   damp scent of mist

   _____

6. lantern glowing brightly
   lantern casting shadows

   _____

7. creaking rusty hinge
   shiny new hinge

   _____

8. wide, graceful stairs
   steep, narrow stairs

   _____

C Details in a description should be in a natural order that makes sense. Here are some examples of natural order:

    tree—bottom to top   surprise package—outside to inside
    costume—top to bottom   stage scene—left to right

Read this prewriting list of details describing a cabin. Decide on a natural order. Write the details in that order on your own paper.

    rusty iron hinges swung open
    cabin appeared spooky in the damp mist
    creaky wooden stairs led to the front door
    whole room inside felt dusty and gloomy
    lantern hung just inside door

Now Think Make prewriting notes for your own paragraph about an old house. Use as many spelling words as you can. First decide what feeling your description will have. Then jot down what you can see through your senses. Finally, decide in what order you will give the details.

Writing. To make a description clear to your reader, use specific details. These details should describe what you see, hear, smell, taste, and feel.

Use Writing Skills

A Complete each set of details with the correct spelling word.

Spelling Words

lamp
stairs
cabin
curtains
stove
hinge
lantern
bucket
mist
scent
dust
pine

Details

blackened, wood-burning _____

damp _____ creeping through the forest

steep _____ with creaking wooden boards

furniture covered with cobwebs and _____

charming, cozy log _____

rusty iron _____ on the door

white lace _____

_____ flickering in the wind

sharp needles of the _____ tree

heavy, metal _____ of sand

tall glass table _____

fragrant _____ of roses

B When you write a rough draft, you will have to expand your prewriting notes into sentences. Practice by expanding each phrase in Column 2 into a complete sentence. Use your own paper.

Example: Dry twigs crackled inside the blackened, wood-burning stove.

Now Write

Look over your prewriting notes. Use them to write a paragraph about an old house. First think of a good topic sentence. Choose details by using your senses. Keep in mind the order in which you will describe things. Also think of the special feeling you want the reader to have. Use as many spelling words as possible.

Revising. One important part of revising is checking to see that you have avoided **run-on sentences.** A run-on sentence contains two or more complete thoughts that are run together.

Example: I tripped on the broken stairs the boards were rotten.
Separate run-on sentences with a punctuation mark. Mark the beginning of every new idea with a capital letter.

Example: I tripped on the broken stairs. The boards were rotten.

Use Revising and Proofreading Skills

A On your own paper, rewrite these run-on sentences correctly.

1. Dad rented a cabin in the woods it was made of logs and cement.

2. Mom shook the dust from the curtains they didn't look so gloomy now.

3. An old wooden bucket stood in the corner the bucket leaked a big puddle of water.

4. A thick mist rose from the ground drops of water clung to the pine needles.

5. There was a fresh scent of spring in the air I skipped happily down the steep front stairs.

B Proofread the following paragraph. Mark all mistakes in capitalization, punctuation, and spelling. Then rewrite the paragraph on your own paper.

Remember
- Use an exclamation point after a statement that shows strong feeling.
- Use an apostrophe to show where letters are left out in a contraction.
- Capitalize the names of people and pets.

Smoke poured from the chimney of the old cabin the wild

wind howled around it. Rita and her dog sandy watched the

sparks dance through the air. Suddenly the wodden roof caught

fire. What a frightening sight that was Rita couldn't see

because of the thick, gloomey smoke. she told sandy theyd have

to go for help.

C Revise the following first draft. Then rewrite it correctly on your own paper. These directions will help you.

1. Underline the sentence that is out of order.
2. Find the punctuation error in line 5.
3. Correct one capitalization error in line 4.
4. Find the run-on sentence. Add a punctuation mark and circle the letter that should be capitalized.
5. Cross out the unnecessary word in line 3.
6. Cross out the six misspelled words. Write them correctly on the lines.

1   One peaceful autumn day Jeff sat outside the caben his family had

2   rented for the week.   After the bug flew away, he looked to the left.   First

3   he watched watched a frendly bug slowly crawling up the sleeve of his

4   jacket.   Then he saw his dog champ pick up the sent of a squirrel in the

5   nearby pine tree.   Ahead, he could see the red glow of a lanturn!   To his

6   right, he saw smoke slowly curling from the chimney next door.   His

7   nieghbor must be using the wood stoave for cooking.   He could almost

8   smell the aroma of her delicious ginger cookies.   Jeff yawned and closed

9   his eyes soon he was snoring.

_____   _____   _____

_____   _____   _____

Now Revise   Now read your own paragraph. Does each sentence tell about the main idea? Did you give details that can be observed through the senses? Are they in a natural order that makes sense? Does your description give a certain feeling to the reader? Have you used the best words? Remember to proofread for mistakes in capitalization, punctuation, and spelling. Then write your final copy in your best handwriting.

You've now written your own description. Trade descriptions with one of your classmates. Notice how each of you sees and describes things in a special, individual way.

A Writer's Journal

The paragraph below was written by a young girl. As you can tell, she has used her writing to express her personal thoughts and feelings. Her paragraph is a good example of one kind of journal entry that you, too, can write.

Read the paragraph in the box carefully. Then discuss the questions with your class.

1. How does the girl explain her changes in mood?

2. How do you think the girl would act when she is in her "good looks mood"? Her "loose end mood"?

3. Often, people have trouble finding the right words to explain what they are feeling or thinking. In your opinion, has the girl found the right words? Why do you feel the way you do?

Now use the paragraph as a starting point for your next journal entry. Here are some ideas for you.

1. Imagine what your mind is like inside. Tell how it looks and how it works.

2. Describe the mood you are in right now. Try to figure out what has caused you to feel the way you do.

MY THOUGHTS

I sometimes wonder what my mind is like inside. Often I fancy that it is like this. I feel as if there is a ball in my mind and it is divided into pieces—each piece stands for a different mood. This ball turns every now and then and that's what makes me change moods. I have my learning mood, my good looks mood, my happy mood, my loose end mood and my grumpy mood, my miserable mood, my thoughtful mood and my planning mood. At the moment I am writing this I am in my thoughtful mood.

—SARAH GRISTWOOD

Building a Personal Word List

Keeping a personal word list can help you become a better speller. First, you can easily see the words you need to learn to spell. Second, you can figure out the kinds of spelling errors you make.

Each time you enter words on your personal list, notice the kinds of spelling errors you made. Maybe you forgot to include the **h** when writing the words **chrome** or **rhyme**. You may begin to notice that you repeat the same kinds of spelling mistakes. If you know what kinds of spelling mistakes you make, you might be able to keep them from happening.

drip	dripped	dripping
grab	grabbed	grabbing
scrub	scrubbed	scrubbing
trip	tripped	tripping
trim	trimmed	trimming
clap	clapped	clapping
drag	dragged	dragging
step	stepped	stepping

1. Look at the words in the first column.
   How many syllables does each word have? _____

   How many vowels are in each word? _____

   How many consonants come at the end of each word? _____

2. The words in the second column are in the past tense.
   What two-letter ending was added to each of these words? _____

   Does the ending begin with a vowel or a consonant? _____
   What happened to the last letter of the base word

   when **ed** was added? _____

3. Look at the words in the last column.
   What three-letter ending was added to these words? _____

   Does the ending begin with a vowel or a consonant? _____
   What happened to the last letter of the base word

   when **ing** was added? _____

Words that have 1 syllable and 1 vowel and end with 1 consonant
   are called **1 + 1 + 1 words**.
Double the final consonant of a **1 + 1 + 1 word** before you add an ending
   that begins with a vowel, such as **ed** or **ing.**

A Complete each sentence with a spelling word. Use either the past tense or the **ing** form.

1. The audience is _____ loudly for the cast of the play.

2. John _____ over a rock and fell down.

3. The ant is _____ the bread crumb across the sidewalk.

4. The shortstop _____ the ball and threw it to home plate.

5. The barber is _____ my brother's hair.

6. I ruined my shoes when I _____ in the wet cement.

7. We called a plumber to fix the _____ faucet.

8. _____ an opponent is against the rules in football.

9. The sailor _____ the deck of the ship.

10. Avoid _____ in the mud.

11. My dog enjoys _____ a frisbee in her mouth.

12. _____ the floor is a tiring job.

13. The men _____ a huge log up the hill.

14. Ben _____ his hands in time with the music.

15. Rain _____ from the roof of our house.

16. The gardener _____ the trees and bushes.

B Unscramble each base word and write it. Then write its **ing** form.

1. prid   _____   _____

2. gard   _____   _____

3. brusc   _____   _____

4. ragb   _____   _____

5. pset   _____   _____

6. iptr   _____   _____

Dictionary

C Write the **ed** form of the spelling words in alphabetical order. Then write the **entry word** that you would look up in the dictionary to find the **ed** form.

1. _____   _____
2. _____   _____
3. _____   _____
4. _____   _____
5. _____   _____
6. _____   _____
7. _____   _____
8. _____   _____

Build Word Power

Writing

Write a sentence to answer each question. Use either the **ed** or **ing** form of the word in parentheses in your sentence.

1. How did Bobby skin his knee?   (trip)

_____

2. Why are you calling the plumber?   (drip)

_____

3. How did you get your sweater dirty?   (drag)

_____

4. What work did you do in the yard today?   (trim)

_____

5. How did you know the audience liked the play?   (clap)

_____

6. Why are your tennis shoes wet?   (step)

_____

dripped	grabbing	tripped	trimming	dragged	stepping
dripping	scrubbed	tripping	clapped	dragging	
grabbed	scrubbing	trimmed	clapping	stepped	

New Words
Discover new words below!

Reach Out for New Words

A Look at the words in each space. Color the space red if the word follows the **1 + 1 + 1** spelling pattern. Color the other spaces blue. Write the words from the red spaces on the lines.

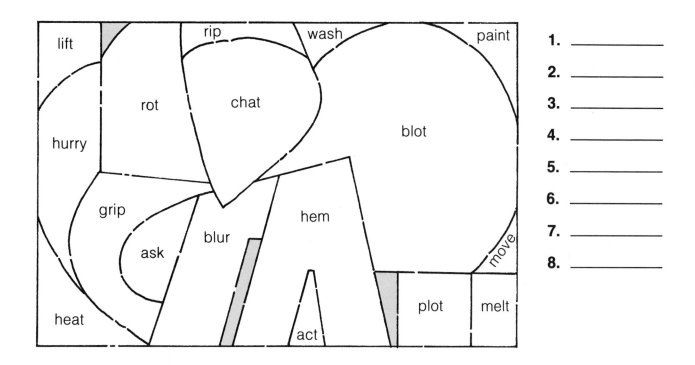

1. _____
2. _____
3. _____
4. _____
5. _____
6. _____
7. _____
8. _____

B Write the eight new **1 + 1 + 1** words in alphabetical order. Then write the past tense and **ing** forms of each word.

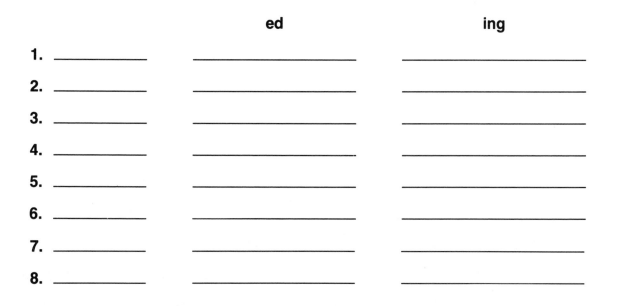

	ed	ing
1.		
2.		
3.		
4.		
5.		
6.		
7.		
8.		

bud	budding	buds
clip	clipping	clips
map	mapping	maps
snap	snapping	snaps
sad	sadder	sadly
thin	thinnest	thinly
ship	shipped	shipment
fit	fitting	fitness

1. The words in the first column have _____ syllable and _____ vowel, and end with _____ consonant. They can be called _____ words.

2. Look at the words in the second column. What endings were added to make these words? _____ _____ _____ _____

   Does each ending begin with a consonant or vowel? _____

   Was the final letter of the base word doubled when an ending was added? _____

3. Look at the words in the third column. What endings were added to make these words? _____ _____ _____ _____

   Does each ending begin with a consonant or a vowel? _____

   Was the final letter of the base word doubled when an ending was added? _____

> Do <u>not</u> double the final consonant of a **1 + 1 + 1 word** when you add an ending that begins with a consonant.

Practice the Words

A Use each clue to find a spelling word that fits in the puzzle.

Across
- **2.** has buds growing
- **4.** unhappily
- **5.** drawings showing towns and streets
- **6.** cutting
- **7.** making something fit
- **9.** slimmest
- **11.** sent something from one place to another

Down
- **1.** making a noise with your fingers
- **3.** things that hold papers together
- **4.** things that are shipped
- **5.** drawing a picture of the earth
- **7.** good health
- **8.** in a thin way
- **10.** small growths that will become flowers or leaves

B Find the misspelled word in each group. Write the word correctly.

1. thinly
buds
sader
snapping

_____

2. clipping
shippment
maps
fitting

_____

3. shipped
clips
snapps
budding

_____

4. buds
mapping
thinest
clips

_____

5. maps
sadley
clipping
shipped

_____

6. thinly
fittness
fitting
mapping

_____

C Write the missing word in each phrase.

1. _____ trees

2. _____ of Michigan, Virginia, and Florida

3. _____ the puzzle pieces together

4. _____ by truck

5. flower _____

6. paper _____

7. the _____ on his jacket

8. _____ sliced bread

9. _____ a route

10. a newspaper _____

11. a _____ story

12. a _____ turtle

Build Word Power

Complete these analogies. Write a word that makes the second pair of words go together in the same way as the first pair. You may use spelling words or their base words.

1. **round** is to **flat**	as	**globe** is to	_____
2. **wide** is to **narrow**	as	**thick** is to	_____
3. **building** is to **strength**	as	**body** is to	_____
4. **grass** is to **sprouting**	as	**flower** is to	_____
5. **letter** is to **mailed**	as	**cargo** is to	_____
6. **happily** is to **gladly**	as	**unhappily** is to	_____
7. **hands** are to **clapping**	as	**fingers** are to	_____
8. **cloth** is to **pins**	as	**paper** is to	_____

budding	clips	snapping	sadly	shipped	fitness
buds	mapping	snaps	thinnest	shipment	
clipping	maps	sadder	thinly	fitting	

New Words

dim	slim
glad	bad
strap	bag
grim	ton
cup	jar

Reach Out for New Words

A Add the endings to each word. Then match each new word to its meaning.

1. cup + ful = _____   a happy feeling

2. slim + ness = _____   being thin

3. dim + ly = _____   as much as a cup will hold

4. glad + ness = _____   very heavy weights

5. ton + s = _____   not brightly

6. bag + ful = _____   narrow strips

7. strap + s = _____   in the wrong way

8. grim + ly = _____   as much as a bag will hold

9. bad + ly = _____   as much as a jar will hold

10. jar + ful = _____   in a harsh way

Dictionary

B Write the new words with the endings in alphabetical order. Look up each word in your spelling dictionary. It may be an entry word, or it may be part of the base word entry. Write all the other forms of the word that are included in the entry.

1. _____   _____

2. _____   _____

3. _____   _____

4. _____   _____

5. _____   _____

6. _____   _____

7. _____   _____

8. _____   _____

9. _____   _____

10. _____   _____

$$hop + ed = hopped$$
$$hope + ed = hoped$$
$$star + ing = starring$$
$$stare + ing = staring$$
$$tap + ed = tapped$$
$$tape + ed = taped$$
$$scar + ed = scarred$$
$$scare + ed = scared$$

$$cut + er = cutter$$
$$cute + er = cuter$$
$$plan + s = plans$$
$$plane + s = planes$$
$$cub + s = cubs$$
$$cube + s = cubes$$
$$tub + ful = tubful$$
$$tube + ful = tubeful$$

1. Some **1 + 1 + 1 words** and final **silent e** words look very much alike.

   The first word in each pair is a _____ word.

   The second word in each pair is a _____ word.

2. Which endings begin with a vowel? _____ _____ _____

   Which endings begin with a consonant? ___ _____

3. What happened to the last letter of the base word

   when **ing**, **ed**, or **er** was added

   to a **1 + 1 + 1 word**? _____ to a **silent e** word? _____

4. What happened to the base word when **s** or **ful** was added

   to a **1 + 1 + 1 word**? _____ to a **silent e** word? _____

When you add an ending that begins with a vowel,
   the base word usually changes.
      The final **e** is dropped in final **silent e** words.
      The final consonant is doubled in **1 + 1 + 1 words**.
When you add an ending that begins with a consonant, the
   base word usually remains the same.

A Complete each sentence with a spelling word.

1. The frightened rabbit _____ toward the woods.

2. My family _____ to go on a picnic this Sunday.

3. The tree trunk is _____ where it was struck by lightning.

4. Kim has always dreamed of _____ in a movie.

5. I _____ a note to the refrigerator door.

6. The paper _____ is very sharp, so be careful when you use it.

7. There are several trays of ice _____ in the freezer.

8. Lynn _____ Bob on the shoulder to get his attention.

9. The monster movie _____ me!

10. Hundreds of _____ land at the airport each day.

11. That little dog is _____ than the big brown one.

12. Sue was _____ at the acrobat on the high wire.

13. The mother bear protected her _____ .

14. Bob ran a _____ of water for his bath.

B Choose the correct spelling of each **base word + ending.** Then write the correct spelling.

1. **cut + er**	cuter	cutter	_____
2. **scare + ed**	scared	scarred	_____
3. **tube + ful**	tubeful	tubful	_____
4. **tap + ed**	tapped	taped	_____
5. **hope + ed**	hoped	hopped	_____
6. **stare + ing**	starring	staring	_____
7. **cute + er**	cutter	cuter	_____
8. **scar + ed**	scared	scarred	_____
9. **star + ing**	starring	staring	_____

C Add the missing letters to complete each word. Then write the base word.

1. t a __ __ d   _____

2. s t __ __ __ n g   _____

3. h o __ __ d   _____

4. c __ __ s   _____

5. t u __ __ __ l   _____

6. p l __ __ s   _____

7. s c __ __ __ d   _____

8. h o __ __ __ d   _____

9. c u __ __ __ r   _____

10. t u __ __ __ __ l   _____

11. p l __ __ __ s   _____

12. c __ __ __ s   _____

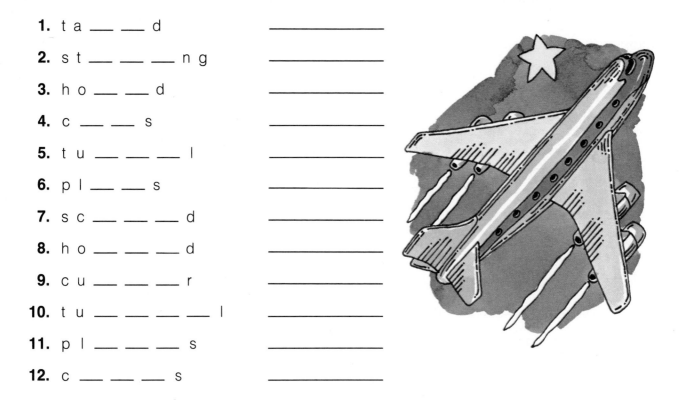

Build Word Power

Writing

Write a sentence with each group of words below. Add an ending to at least one word in each sentence. Remember to think about the **1 + 1 + 1** and final **silent e** patterns when you add endings.

1. cute, stare, star _____

   _____

2. plan, hope, plane _____

   _____

3. tape, cut, tube _____

   _____

4. hop, scare, cub _____

   _____

94

hopped	staring	scarred	cuter	cubs	tubeful
hoped	tapped	scared	plans	cubes	
starring	taped	cutter	planes	tubful	

New Words

rob	robe
mop	mope
scrap	scrape

Reach Out for New Words

A Unscramble each group of letters to make a word. Then add the ending to each word. Check the spelling in the dictionary, and write the new word form.

1. peom   _____   +   ed   =   _____

2. opm   _____   +   ed   =   _____

3. orb   _____   +   ed   =   _____

4. boer   _____   +   ed   =   _____

5. praces   _____   +   s   =   _____

6. rascp   _____   +   s   =   _____

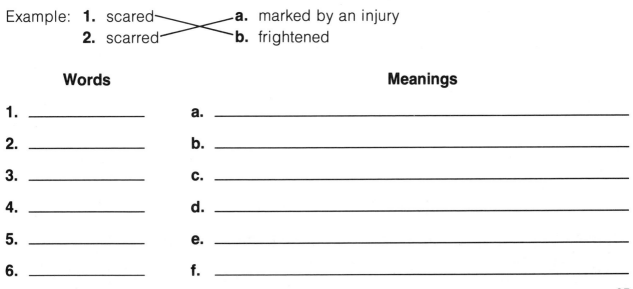

B Write each new base word in the first column. Write the meaning of each word in the second column so that it is *not* across from the correct word. Ask a friend to draw a line from each word to its meaning.

Example: **1.** scared   **a.** marked by an injury
          2. scarred   **b.** frightened

Words   **Meanings**

1. _____   **a.** _____

2. _____   **b.** _____

3. _____   **c.** _____

4. _____   **d.** _____

5. _____   **e.** _____

6. _____   **f.** _____

95

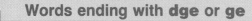

badge
edge
bridge
dodge
fudge
judge

page
huge
stage
fringe
sponge
strange
garage
orange
arrange

1. Look at the first group of words.
   How many syllables does each word have? _____

   What are the last three letters of each word? _____
   Does a consonant or a vowel come before these letters? _____

   Is the vowel long or short? _____
2. Look at the second group of words.
   What are the last two letters of each word? _____

> Use **dge** immediately after a single, short vowel in a one-syllable word.
> Use **ge** in most other words.

A Use each clue to find the spelling words that fit in the boxes.

1. part of a book

2. a color

3. get out of the way

4. used to clean up spills

5. a border of hanging threads

6. keep a car in it

7. very large

8. where plays are performed

9. border

10. It goes over a river.

11. to put in order

12. a person who decides cases in a court of law

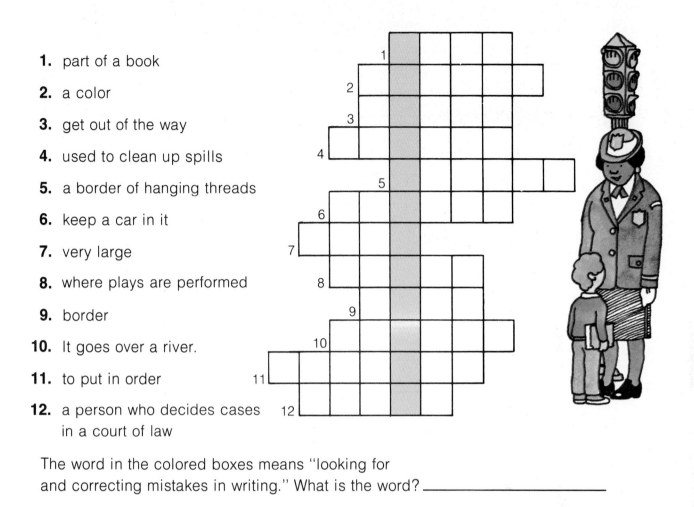

The word in the colored boxes means "looking for and correcting mistakes in writing." What is the word? _____

Proofreading

B Proofread this paragraph. Five of the words are misspelled. Find each misspelled word and write it correctly.

   While working on a cooking bage for scouts, Jan and I made a huge batch of fudg. We found the recipe on padge fifteen of the cookbook. Jan got out the cocoa, salt, milk, butter, and vanilla. I got out a bowl, a mixer, and a spunge for cleaning up. As we mixed the ingredients, Jan took a taste from the edge of the bowl. He made a strang face. We had forgotten to add the sugar!

1. _____ 3. _____ 5. _____

2. _____ 4. _____

Dictionary

Each dictionary entry includes an abbreviation that tells you the part of speech of the entry word. Some parts of speech and their abbreviations are:

noun—*n.*   verb—*v.*   adjective—*adj.*

Some words have more than one part of speech listed in the entry.

huge (hyōōj) *adj.* very large _____ part of speech

judge (juj) *n.* an official who hears cases in a
law court and makes decisions on them
—*pl.* **judg' es** ♦*v.* to hear cases and make
decisions in a law court
⎫
⎬ parts of speech
⎭

C Write your spelling words in alphabetical order. Look up each word in the dictionary. Write the abbreviation for the part or parts of speech you find in the entry.

1. _____ _____   9. _____ _____

2. _____ _____   10. _____ _____

3. _____ _____   11. _____ _____

4. _____ _____   12. _____ _____

5. _____ _____   13. _____ _____

6. _____ _____   14. _____ _____

7. _____ _____   15. _____ _____

8. _____ _____

Build Word Power

Each word below is part of a spelling word. Write the spelling word on the line. Do not use a spelling word more than once.

1. rag _____   7. rid _____

2. tag _____   8. on _____

3. age _____   9. do _____

4. bad _____   10. or _____

5. ring _____   11. rang _____

6. hug _____   12. range _____

badge	dodge	page	fringe	garage
edge	fudge	huge	sponge	orange
bridge	judge	stage	strange	arrange

Reach Out for New Words

A Words are printed in three directions in this puzzle. → ↓ ↘
Find three new **ge** words and four new **dge** words. Circle each word and write it.

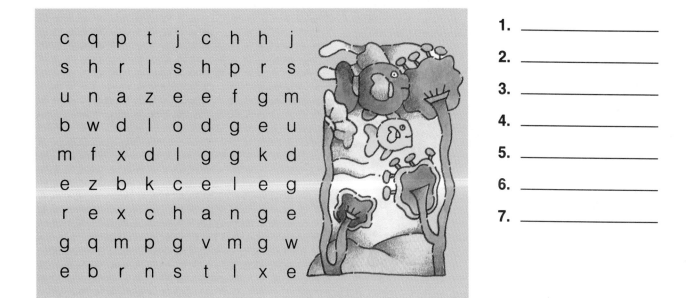

```
c q p t j c h h j
s h r l s h p r s
u n a z e e f g m
b w d l o d g e u
m f x d l g g k d
e z b k c e l e g
r e x c h a n g e
g q m p g v m g w
e b r n s t l x e
```

1. _____
2. _____
3. _____
4. _____
5. _____
6. _____
7. _____

B Use each clue to find one of the new words that fits in the puzzle.

Across
4. a dirty spot
7. dare

Down
1. a cabin
2. to put under water
3. trade
5. promise
6. a row of bushes

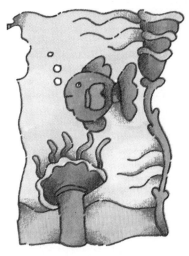

catch
patch
sketch
stretch
pitch
witch
ditch

touch
peach
beach
bench
march
sandwich
spinach
attach

1. Look at the first group of words.
   How many syllables does each word have? _____

   What are the last three letters of each word? _____
   Does a consonant or a vowel come before these letters? _____

   Is the vowel long or short? _____

2. Look at the second group of words.
   What are the last two letters of each word?. _____

Use **tch** immediately after a single, short vowel in a one-syllable word.
Use **ch** in most other words.

Practice the Words

A Use each clue to find a spelling word that fits in the puzzle.

Across

1. to draw
3. a long seat
5. a popular Halloween costume
7. to throw
9. to fasten together
10. to pull out of shape
11. to mend by adding a piece
12. a sandy shore
13. a steady walk

Down

1. slices of bread with filling between them
2. to capture
4. a green vegetable
6. to feel with the hand
8. a trench by a road
11. a fruit

B Complete each sentence with spelling words that rhyme.

1. Mark ate a juicy _peach_ while sitting on the _____.

2. Try not to _____ the ball in the _____.

3. I will _____ out on the grass and _____ a picture.

4. Please _____ a _____ to these jeans before

   I _____ a cold!

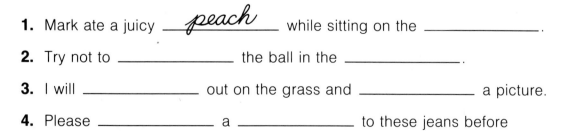

Dictionary

Each dictionary entry tells the meaning, or **definition**, of the entry word.

C Write these words in alphabetical order. Look up each word in your spelling dictionary and write the definition.

witch   touch   peach   bench   sandwich   march   spinach

1. _____ _____

2. _____ _____

3. _____ _____

4. _____ _____

5. _____ _____

6. _____ _____

7. _____ _____

Build Word Power

Writing

Write a sentence with each group of words below. You may add the endings **ed**, **ing**, or **er** to some of the words if you wish.

1. pitch, catch, ditch _____

_____

2. stretch, beach, sandwich _____

_____

3. bench, sketch, peach _____

_____

4. attach, patch, march _____

_____

5. spinach, touch, witch _____

_____

catch	stretch	ditch	beach	sandwich
patch	pitch	touch	bench	spinach
sketch	witch	peach	march	attach

New Words

crutch	approach
ostrich	drench
switch	fetch
scratch	stitch

Reach Out for New Words

Dictionary

A Fill in **ch** or **tch** in each word below. Remember to use **tch** after a single, short vowel in a one-syllable word. Look up each word in your spelling dictionary. Write the word, the number of syllables, and the part or parts of speech.

	Word	Syllables	Part(s) of speech
1. cru __tch__	_crutch_	_1_	_n._
2. approa _____	_____	_____	_____
3. sti _____	_____	_____	_____
4. swi _____	_____	_____	_____
5. dren _____	_____	_____	_____
6. ostri _____	_____	_____	_____
7. fe _____	_____	_____	_____
8. scra _____	_____	_____	_____

B Use the clues to write each new word that fits in the boxes. Then use the letters in the numbered boxes to fill in the blanks that answer the riddle.

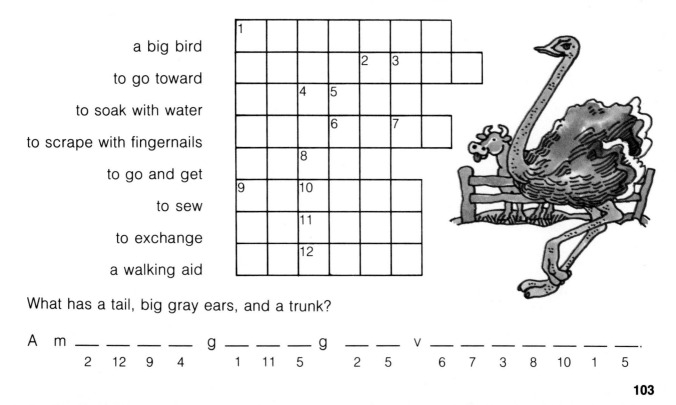

a big bird

to go toward

to soak with water

to scrape with fingernails

to go and get

to sew

to exchange

a walking aid

What has a tail, big gray ears, and a trunk?

A m __ __ __ __ g __ __ __ g __ __ v __ __ __ __ __ __ __ __.
   2 12 9 4   1 11 5   2 5   6 7 3 8 10 1 5

bush + es = bushes
leash + es = leashes
branch + es = branches
match + es = matches
ax + es = axes
waitress + es = waitresses
boss + es = bosses
circus + es = circuses

case + es = cases
fence + es = fences
chance + es = chances
sentence + es = sentences
sneeze + es = sneezes
breeze + es = breezes
package + es = packages

1. The eight words in the first column are all singular nouns. How many words

   end with **sh**? _____ with **ch**? _____ with **x**? _____ with **s**? _____

2. The seven **silent e** words are also singular nouns.

   How many end with **se**? _____ with **ce**? _____ with **ze**? _____ with **ge**? _____

3. What ending was added to each singular noun to make the plural form? _____

4. What happened to the **silent e** when **es** was added? _____

5. Say the plural nouns. Each plural word has _____ more syllable than its
   singular form.

When a word ends with **sh**, **ch**, **x**, or **s**, add **es** to make the plural form.
When a word ends with **se**, **ce**, **ze**, or **ge**, drop the **e** and add **es**
     to make the plural form.
A plural word that ends with **es** has one more syllable than its singular form.

A Write the spelling words that complete these sentences.

1. Clowns and trapeze artists perform at most _____ .

2. The lumberjacks are using sharp _____ to chop wood.

3. The _____ served lunch to the customers.

4. All our neighbors have _____ around their yards.

5. Summer _____ help us keep cool.

6. The wind storm knocked four _____ off our tree.

7. Two big _____ arrived in the mail today.

8. Don wrote five _____ about the story.

9. I need _____ to light these candles.

10. Pat is trimming the _____ in our yard.

11. Our dogs enjoy going for walks on their _____ .

12. Smelling pepper often causes _____ .

B Find the misspelled word in each group. Write the word correctly.

1. fences	2. leashes	3. chanses
caces	branches	waitresses
sneezes	maches	bushes
axes	breezes	sentences

_____   _____   _____

4. waitresses	5. sneezes	6. fences
breezes	boses	sentences
leashes	bushes	circusses
pakages	axes	branches

_____   _____   _____

C Add the missing vowels to complete each word. Then write its base word.

1. s n __ __ z __ s _____

2. b __ s s __ s _____

3. b __ s h __ s _____

4. __ x __ s _____

5. c __ s __ s _____

6. f __ n c __ s _____

7. c h __ n c __ s _____

8. b r __ __ z __ s _____

9. c __ r c __ s __ s _____

10. b r __ n c h __ s _____

11. p __ c k __ g __ s _____

12. l __ __ s h __ s _____

13. w __ __ t r __ s s __ s _____

14. m __ t c h __ s _____

15. s __ n t __ n c __ s _____

Build Word Power

Each underlined word goes with one or more of your spelling words. Write the spelling word. Then write a sentence using both words.

1. Fire goes with _____.

_____

2. Clowns go with _____.

_____

3. Chopping goes with _____.

_____

4. Restaurants go with _____.

_____

5. Ribbons go with _____.

_____

6. Words go with _____.

_____

7. Trees go with _____.

_____

bushes	matches	bosses	fences	sneezes
leashes	axes	circuses	chances	breezes
branches	waitresses	cases	sentences	packages

New Words

Discover new words below!

Reach Out for New Words

A Find the correct path through this maze. Words that add **es** to make the plural form are on the correct path. Write the ten words that are on the correct path.

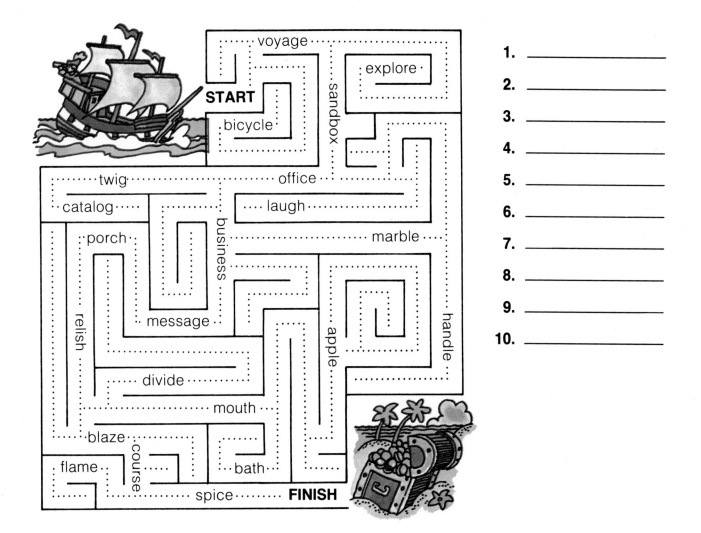

1. _____

2. _____

3. _____

4. _____

5. _____

6. _____

7. _____

8. _____

9. _____

10. _____

B Write the plural form of each new word you found in the maze.

1. _____   6. _____

2. _____   7. _____

3. _____   8. _____

4. _____   9. _____

5. _____   10. _____

nature

picture

capture

creature

future

fracture

pasture

mixture

lecture

signature

departure

furniture

adventure

temperature

manufacture

What are the last four letters of each word? _____

Many words end with the letters **ture.**

Practice the Words

A Write your spelling words in alphabetical order. Then circle the word or phrase in the sentence with almost the same meaning as the spelling word.

1. _____ Exploring a cave is an exciting event.

2. _____ Did the zoo keeper catch the lion?

3. _____ A tiger is a beautiful living being.

4. _____ The plane's leaving was delayed by snow.

5. _____ Nick didn't break his arm when he fell out of the tree.

6. _____ We bought new chairs and tables for our living room.

7. _____ I hope to travel in space in the time to come.

8. _____ The teacher gave a speech on sea life.

9. _____ What do they make in that factory?

10. _____ Hot chocolate is a combination of milk, sugar, and cocoa.

11. _____ Fred hopes to become a famous outdoor photographer.

12. _____ The cows are grazing in the field.

13. _____ Ann took a photograph of the White House.

14. _____ Is the artist's signed name on the painting?

15. _____ Did the weather forecaster predict the degree of coldness for tomorrow?

B Write the spelling word that goes with each word or phrase.

1. exploring a sunken ship _____

2. a chair _____

3. *John Smith* _____

4. a broken leg _____

5. 1999 _____

6. 75 degrees _____

Dictionary

C Write these words in alphabetical order. Then look up each word in your spelling dictionary and write the definition.

capture   pasture   lecture   manufacture   temperature   mixture

1. _____   _____

2. _____   _____

3. _____   _____

4. _____   _____

5. _____   _____

6. _____   _____

Build Word Power

Writing

Read each pair of sentences. Put the two sentences together to make one sentence that includes the underlined spelling word.

1. The teacher gave a lecture. The lecture was on early American settlers.

_____

2. Mr. Clark bought some furniture. The furniture is made of oak.

_____

3. Alice took a picture. The picture is of our family.

_____

4. The cows are in the pasture. The pasture is behind the barn.

_____

5. Jill stirred the mixture. The mixture is of butter, sugar, and eggs.

_____

6. Terry enjoyed his adventure. His adventure was on board the ship.

_____

nature   creature   pasture   signature   adventure
picture   future   mixture   departure   temperature
capture   fracture   lecture   furniture   manufacture

New Words
fixture
culture
posture
miniature
feature
agriculture
legislature
puncture

Reach Out for New Words

A Add the missing consonants to complete each word.
Then write the word.

1. __ ea __ u __ e   _____

2. __ e __ i __ __ a __ u __ e   _____

3. __ u __ __ __ u __ e   _____

4. __ i __ __ u __ e   _____

5. a __ __ i __ u __ __ u __ e   _____

6. __ o __ __ u __ e   _____

7. __ u __ __ u __ e   _____

8. __ i __ ia __ u __ e   _____

B Write the spelling words that complete these sentences.

1. Her eyes are the most beautiful _____ of her face.

2. Joshua has a collection of _____ cars.

3. Driving over a nail can _____ a tire.

4. It is interesting to study the _____ of other countries.

5. Improve your _____ by standing up straight.

6. The _____ of our country makes laws.

7. People who study _____ learn about farming.

8. A light _____ hangs above the dining room table.

19

drip   dripped   dripping
trim   trimmed   trimming
clap   clapped   clapping

20

sad   sadly
ship   shipment
fit   fitness

21

hop   hopped
hope   hoped
tape   taped

22

fudge
huge
orange

23

catch
peach
sandwich

24

bush   bushes
branch   branches
package   packages

25

picture
future
temperature

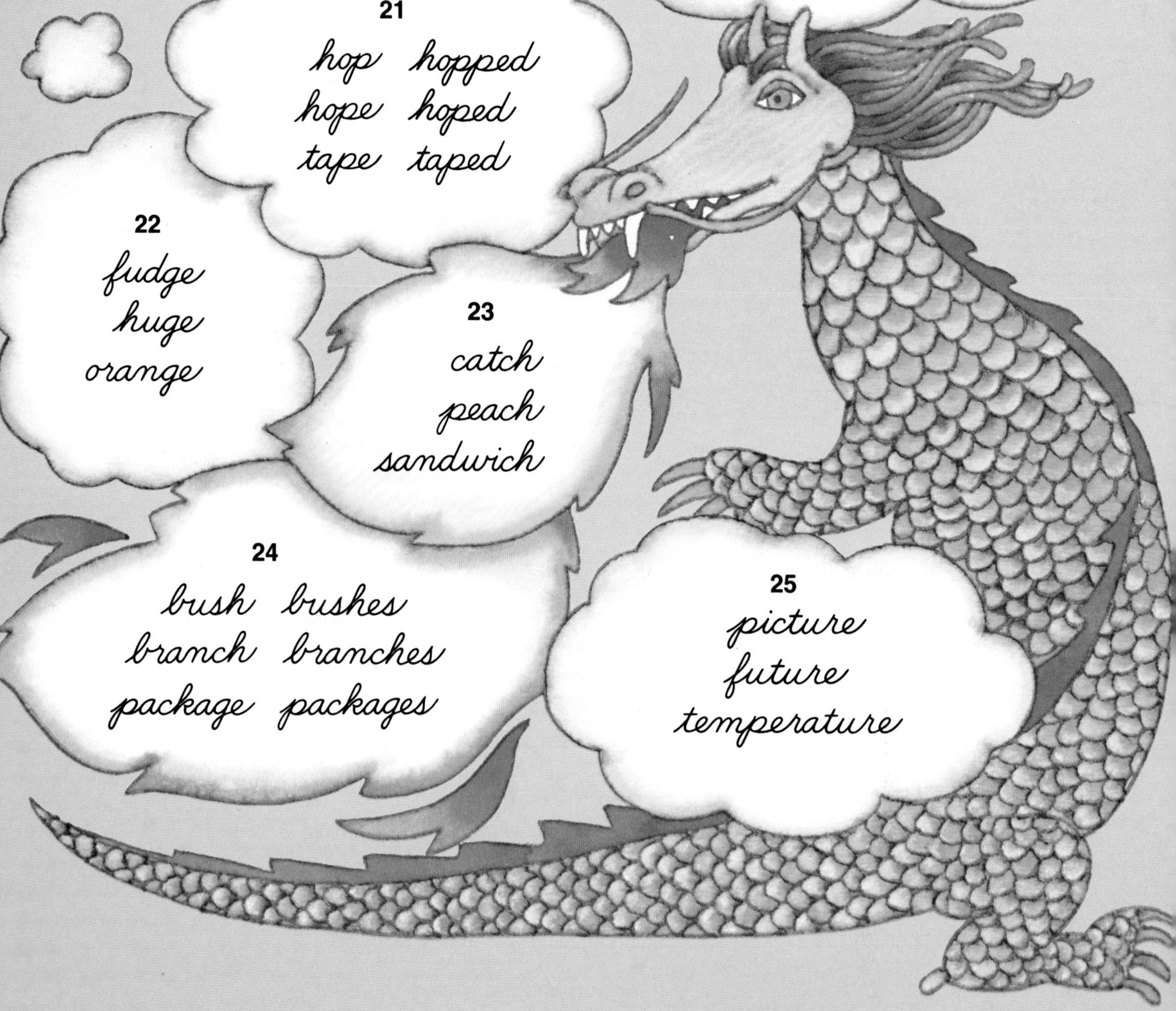

Using Review Words

A Complete these analogies. Write the spelling word that makes the second pair of words go together in the same way as the first pair.

1. **trim** is to **trimming**   as   **drip** is to   _____

2. **thin** is to **thinly**   as   **sad** is to   _____

3. **hope** is to **hoped**   as   **tape** is to   _____

4. **trip** is to **tripped**   as   **clap** is to   _____

5. **sandwich** is to **sandwiches**   as   **branch** is to   _____

6. **tap** is to **tapped**   as   **hop** is to   _____

7. **fitness** is to **fit**   as   **shipment** is to   _____

8. **taped** is to **tape**   as   **hoped** is to   _____

9. **oranges** is to **orange**   as   **packages** is to   _____

10. **scrubbed** is to **scrub**   as   **trimmed** is to   _____

Proofreading

B Cross out each misspelled word. Write the word correctly.

1. Carla raked the leaves and trimed the bushs.

_____

2. In the fuchure, I will improve my physical fittness.

_____

3. Jane ate a hudge bowl of fudge ripple ice cream.

_____

4. These packages must be taped well for shippment.

_____

5. Max hopped that Kate would give him a peech.

_____

6. The rabbit hoped quickly into the woods.

_____

C Complete each phrase with a word from the box.

picture	fudge	fitness	orange	temperature
sandwich	clapped	bushes	future	catch

1. _____ juice

2. _____ their hands

3. chocolate _____

4. _____ the ball

5. ham and cheese _____

6. painting a _____

7. _____ of 32°F

8. predict the _____

9. physical _____

10. trim the _____

Using More Review Words

A Use the directions following each base word to make another form of the word.

1. thin   write the **ly** form   _____

2. thin   write the **est** form   _____

3. scrub   write the past tense   _____

4. leash   write the plural   _____

5. step   write the **ing** form   _____

6. sad   write the **er** form   _____

7. fit   write the **ing** form   _____

8. cut   write the **er** form   _____

9. waitress   write the plural   _____

10. trip   write the past tense   _____

11. sentence   write the plural   _____

12. tub   write the **ful** form   _____

13. breeze   write the plural   _____

14. drag   write the **ing** form   _____

15. circus   write the plural   _____

B Three words in each row follow the same spelling pattern. One word does not.
Find that word. Be ready to tell why it does not belong.

1. touch   leash   beach   bench

2. page   badge   garage   arrange

3. scared   grabbed   clapped   scarred

4. nature   capture   pasture   stare

5. buds   fences   maps   snaps

6. bosses   axes   clips   matches

7. sentences   cases   chances   plans

8. stretch   drag   step   plan

9. attach   patch   witch   sketch

10. hoped   staring   tripping   cuter

C Complete these analogies. Write a word from the box that makes the second
pair of words go together in the same way as the first pair.

beach	departure	planes	tubeful	stepping
axes	pitch	cubs	garage	spinach

1. **fingers** are to **snapping**   as   **feet** are to   _____

2. **football** is to **pass**   as   **baseball** is to   _____

3. **come** is to **go**   as   **arrival** is to   _____

4. **jam** is to **jarful**   as   **toothpaste** is to   _____

5. **sheep** are to **lambs**   as   **bears** are to   _____

6. **cutting** is to **saws**   as   **chopping** is to   _____

7. **river** is to **bank**   as   **ocean** is to   _____

8. **drive** is to **buses**   as   **fly** is to   _____

9. **airplane** is to **hangar**   as   **car** is to   _____

10. **fruit** is to **apple**   as   **vegetable** is to   _____

brand   facts   plenty   vitamins
money   ideas   healthy   cheaper
smart   goes   getting   product
truth   sale   forever   whether
until   cents   cereal   opinion

Prewriting. Prewriting is the thinking and planning you do before you begin to write. In this lesson, you are going to plan and write a **paragraph that explains why.** You will give reasons for an opinion.

Use Prewriting Skills

A Answer the questions with spelling words. The words will help you think of ideas for writing an ad or commercial for your favorite food.

1. What word means something that is made? _____

2. What word means the name on the label of a product? _____

3. What words might you use to talk about costs? _____

_____   _____   _____

4. What products can you buy at the grocery store?

_____   _____

5. What should an honest advertisement tell? _____   _____

6. What word means "all that one needs"? _____

7. What should good food help you become? _____

8. When you say what brand you think is best, what are you

stating? _____

B In a paragraph that explains why, you must give reasons. These reasons must be facts, not opinions. Facts can be proven right or wrong. Opinions cannot be proven. Read the six sentences below. Write three that are **opinions.**

1. Meowies Cat Food goes on sale today until Monday.

2. Shoppers with smart ideas should buy Meowies.

3. Once you buy Meowies, you will buy it forever.

4. Your pet will be getting vitamins and protein in its food.

5. Pets, whether young or old, should be fed Meowies.

6. Meowies is a product made from meat and natural foods.

1. _____

2. _____

3. _____

C Plan to present your facts in order from the least to the most important. That way, your reader will be left with the strongest reason. Write the facts from Activity B in order from the least to the most important.

1. _____

2. _____

3. _____

Now Think   Make prewriting notes for your own magazine ad or TV commercial. Write about a food product such as cereal. Choose facts that will convince people to buy your product. Make up an imaginary brand name. Use as many spelling words as you can in your paragraph.

Writing. When you write to explain why, begin with a **topic sentence** that states your opinion. Then support your opinion with a set of facts.

Use Writing Skills

A Write three different topic sentences that state opinions. Use the words in parentheses in each. Remember that opinions cannot be proven right or wrong.

1. (vitamins, healthy) _____

_____

2. (smart, brand) _____

_____

3. (product, cheaper) _____

_____

B Do not combine more than two thoughts in one sentence. A sentence with three or more complete thoughts is called a **stringy sentence.**
   Example: Spotless Pans are made of metal and they have a non-stick surface and they are dishwasher safe.

Correct a stringy sentence by breaking it into at least two shorter sentences. Leave out one or more of the **and**'s. You may leave some ideas combined if they have a lot in common.
   Example: Spotless Pans are made of metal and they have a non-stick surface. They are dishwasher safe.

Rewrite these stringy sentences on your own paper. Be careful to use capital letters, commas, end marks, and connecting words in the right places.

1. Wisebuys is a paper that prints facts about new products and it gives good ideas on how to stay healthy and it only costs ninety cents.
2. You can find all brands of vitamins at the Smart Shop and we are open twenty-four hours a day and we even deliver.

Now Write Use your prewriting notes to write an ad or commercial for a food product. Begin with a topic sentence that tells why your product is good. Then give facts that support your topic sentence. Arrange your facts from the least to the most important. Use as many spelling words as possible.

Revising. When you revise a paragraph that explains why, make sure that all your details are facts. These facts should support your topic sentence.

Use Revising and Proofreading Skills

A In the following paragraph cross out two details that don't support the topic sentence. Also underline one reason that is an opinion, not a fact. Rewrite the paragraph on your own paper.

Whether you feel healthy or not, you need to take Aunty Flynn's Vitamins every day. The Aunty Flynn brand is now over twenty years old. Aunty Flynn's has both Vitamin A and Vitamin C. It also contains minerals such as iron. Our vitamins are the best by far! Aunty Flynn's comes in a red box. Aunty Flynn's provides you with a daily supply of all the necessary vitamins.

B Proofread the following facts for mistakes in capitalization, punctuation, and spelling. Then write the sentences correctly.

Remember
- Use a comma before the word *and* when it connects two thoughts in a sentence.
- Do not combine more than two thoughts in a sentence.
- Capitalize brand names.

1. chewies is a new brand of sugarless gum. It helps to keep your mouth helthy and it adds plentey of shine to your teeth.

_____

_____

2. the big sale of supersuds Soap begins today and it will last until Friday during this time it will be cheiper than most other brands.

_____

_____

C Revise the following first draft. The directions below will help you. Then make a corrected copy on your own paper.

1. Cross out one reason that is an opinion, not a fact.
2. Correct one stringy sentence. Add a period and a capital letter. Cross out one **and.**
3. Cross out six misspelled words. Write them correctly on the lines.
4. Correct the capitalization errors in lines 1 and 7.
5. Correct the punctuation errors in lines 1 and 5.

1 Laser Lights teaching Computer, is the best home computer ever

2 manufractured. It was designed by a team of engineers, teachers, and

3 students. This produck's memory center has all the facts you will need

4 and it has a homework input device, and their's a printer to deliver your

5 finished copy. Laser Lights works on laser beams and, that's why it's

6 cheeper to run than many other computers. This computer will look good

7 in your home. Most importantly, Laser lights is guaranteed farever. Call

8 555-2626 unntil midnight for more information. A salesperson will be glad

9 to give you a demonstration in your own home.

_____   _____   _____

_____   _____   _____

Now Revise   Read your own ad or commercial for a food product. Does your topic sentence give an opinion? Have you given at least three facts to back up the topic sentence? Are the facts stated in clear, short sentences? Check to make sure your statements are facts, not opinions. Then proofread for mistakes in capitalization, punctuation, and spelling. Make a final copy in your best handwriting.

Plan to read your paragraph aloud. Others will enjoy hearing how you have used the process of writing to express and support your opinion.

Read the poem. Think about what it means. Then discuss the questions with your class.

1. At the first picnic were there really "tigers behind every boulder"?

2. By the second picnic, years later, what had changed? Had the rocks become smaller?

Maybe the poem or the discussion has given you a good idea for your next journal entry. If so, begin writing. If not, you might want to use one of the ideas given below.

1. Tell about a time when you imagined something scary. You might tell about something that happened a long time ago or something that happened recently. Try to figure out why you were scared.

2. Describe how you felt on your first day of school this year. Have your feelings changed between then and now? If so, why do you think they have changed? Answer these questions in your journal.

Building a Personal Word List

Your personal word list contains all the words that gave you trouble. Now that you know the words you need to practice, how can you go about learning these words? You could try one of these ways.

1. Look carefully at the words on your list. Do any of them look like words you know how to spell? Knowing how to spell **temperature** may help you spell **literature.**

2. Look for patterns. Do any of the words on your list have familiar spelling patterns? You might notice, for example, that **cases, fences,** and **breezes** all drop the silent **e** before the ending **es** is added. Practice spelling the words as a group.

GROWING UP

When I was seven
We went for a picnic
Up to a magic
Foresty place.
I knew there were tigers
Behind every boulder,
Though I didn't meet one
Face to face.

When I was older
We went for a picnic
Up to the very same
Place as before,
And all of the trees
And the rocks were so little
They couldn't hide tigers
Or *me* any more.

—HARRY BEHN

un + hurt	=	unhurt
un + fold	=	unfold
un + known	=	unknown
un + popular	=	unpopular
un + welcome	=	unwelcome
un + important	=	unimportant
un + lawful	=	unlawful
un + friendly	=	unfriendly
un + selfish	=	unselfish
un + aware	=	unaware
un + fastened	=	unfastened
un + usual	=	unusual
in + complete	=	incomplete
in + correct	=	incorrect
in + expensive	=	inexpensive

A **prefix** is a group of letters added to the beginning of a word to change its meaning.

1. What prefix was added to twelve of the base words? _____

2. What prefix was added to three of the base words? _____

3. Was the spelling of the base word changed when **un** or **in** was added? _____

The prefixes **un** and **in** mean *not* or *the opposite of*.
Do <u>not</u> change the spelling of the base word when a prefix is added.

    un + fold = unfold = the opposite of fold
    un + important = unimportant = not important
    in + correct = incorrect = not correct

Practice the Words

A The underlined words in each sentence have the same meaning as one of your spelling words. Write the spelling word.

1. My report is <u>not finished</u>. _____

2. Dad fell off the ladder, but he was <u>not injured</u>. _____

3. Anita is always <u>thoughtful of others</u>. _____

4. Please <u>spread out</u> the map so we can read it. _____

5. This type of music is <u>not liked by most people</u>. _____

6. These shirts are <u>not costly</u>. _____

7. Robbing banks is <u>not legal</u>. _____

8. The strange man was <u>not pleasant or agreeable</u>. _____

9. Mosquitoes are <u>not gladly allowed</u> in our house. _____

10. Your answer to this math problem is <u>wrong</u>. _____

11. This information was <u>of little value</u> to us. _____

12. The name of the person who wrote this poem is <u>not something we know</u>. _____

13. A solar eclipse is a <u>rare</u> event. _____

14. Todd <u>opened</u> the snaps on his jacket. _____

B Look at each word. If it is spelled correctly, draw a ☺. If it is misspelled, write the correct spelling.

1. unpopullar _____

2. unimportant _____

3. innexpensive _____

4. unlawfull _____

5. incorect _____

6. unusual _____

7. unfreindly _____

8. incorrect _____

9. unselfish _____

10. inccomplete _____

11. unawear _____

12. unfasened _____

Dictionary

C Write your **un** spelling words in alphabetical order. Then look up each word in the dictionary and divide it into syllables.

1. _unaware_   _un•a•ware_
2. _____   _____
3. _____   _____
4. _____   _____
5. _____   _____
6. _____   _____
7. _____   _____
8. _____   _____
9. _____   _____
10. _____   _____
11. _____   _____
12. _____   _____

Build Word Power

Make at least three new words from each spelling word below by adding or subtracting prefixes and endings. You may use these endings: **s**, **ed**, **ing**, **ly**, and **less**.

1. unfold _____

_____

2. unwelcome _____

_____

3. unlawful _____

_____

4. unfriendly _____

_____

5. incomplete _____

_____

unhurt	unpopular	unlawful	unaware	incomplete
unfold	unwelcome	unfriendly	unfastened	incorrect
unknown	unimportant	unselfish	unusual	inexpensive

New Words
Discover new words below!

Reach Out for New Words

A Circle every other letter in each group below to find six new **un** words and two new **in** words. Always start by circling the second letter. Write the new words.

1. n(i)a(n)m(d)r(i)e(g)b(e)n(s)e(t)l(i)(o)a(n)
2. a u i n c n r e a c m e v s e s c a h r i y
3. s u i n o e r x t p s e l c b t a e c d
4. c u o n g s h a c t d i n s a f l a n c r t f o n r b y
5. o i g n r c a o v n l s y i s d n e p r x a e t t e
6. n u e n l f l i a n v i o s l h r e m d
7. t u i n a p m r h e s p n a w r o e t d
8. c u i n l i a n d t n e a r l e r s d t n i o n w g

1. _____   5. _____

2. _____   6. _____

3. _____   7. _____

4. _____   8. _____

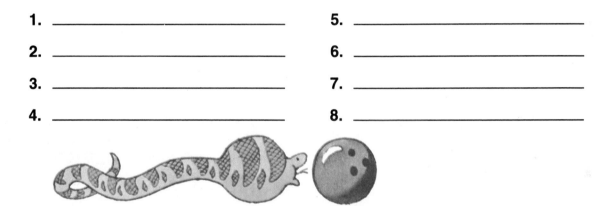

B Write the new word that matches each meaning.

1. not needed   _____

2. not complete   _____

3. not good enough   _____

4. surprising   _____

5. difficulty in digesting food   _____

6. not of interest   _____

7. not ready   _____

8. not thinking of others   _____

mis + spell = *misspell*
mis + understand = *misunderstand*
mis + behave = *misbehave*
mis + lead = *mislead*
mis + print = *misprint*
mis + lay = *mislay*
mis + read = *misread*
mis + used = *misused*

dis + obey = *disobey*
dis + arm = *disarm*
dis + like = *dislike*
dis + honest = *dishonest*
dis + please = *displease*
dis + loyal = *disloyal*
dis + connect = *disconnect*

1. A group of letters that is added to the beginning of a word to change its meaning is called a _____.
2. What two prefixes were added to the base words to make the words in the last column? _____ _____
3. Was the spelling of the base word changed when the prefix was added? _____

The prefix **mis** means *bad* or *wrongly*.
The prefix **dis** means *not* or *to do the opposite*.
Do <u>not</u> change the spelling of the base word when a prefix is added.
    mis + spell = misspell = to spell wrongly
    dis + obey = disobey = to not obey
    dis + connect = disconnect = the opposite of connect

Practice the Words

A Use each clue to find a spelling word that fits in the puzzle. The letter **s** has been given to help you.

1. to put in the wrong place
2. to take away weapons
3. used in the wrong way
4. lead in the wrong direction
5. not do as you are told
6. not enjoy
7. to read the wrong way
8. not faithful
9. to spell incorrectly
10. a mistake in printing
11. make someone angry
12. not truthful
13. to act badly
14. to break a connection
15. not get the meaning

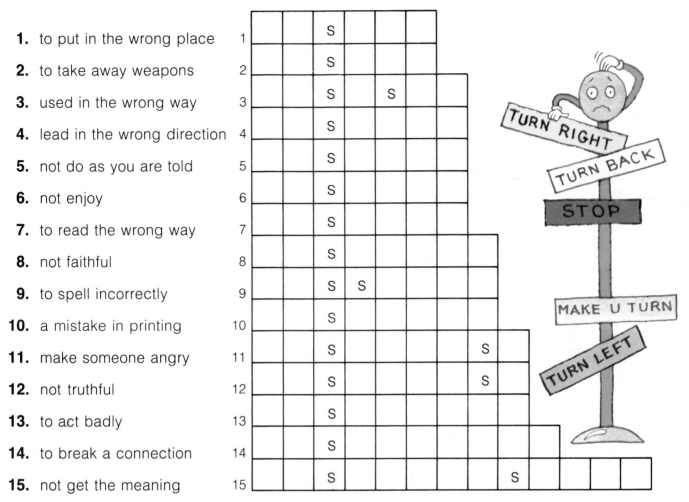

B Find the misspelled word in each group. Write the word correctly.

1. discconect
   disloyal
   mislead
   _____

2. dislike
   missunderstand
   misbehave
   _____

3. disarm
   mispell
   misprint
   _____

4. disarm
   mislay
   disonest
   _____

5. misused
   misread
   displeese
   _____

6. misbehave
   disobay
   disloyal
   _____

Dictionary

C Write your spelling words in alphabetical order. Remember to look at the fourth or fifth letter if the first letters are the same. Then look up each word in your spelling dictionary and write its part of speech.

1. _____ _____
2. _____ _____
3. _____ _____
4. _____ _____
5. _____ _____
6. _____ _____
7. _____ _____

8. _____ _____
9. _____ _____
10. _____ _____
11. _____ _____
12. _____ _____
13. _____ _____
14. _____ _____
15. _____ _____

Build Word Power

The words in the box are base forms of your spelling words. Use the clues to make new forms of these words. Make each new form by adding an ending or by adding both a prefix and an ending. Use the prefixes **mis** and **dis** and the endings **ly**, **ed**, and **s**. Write the new word forms that fit in the puzzle.

honest	like	behave	please	loyal
connect	lay	read	print	

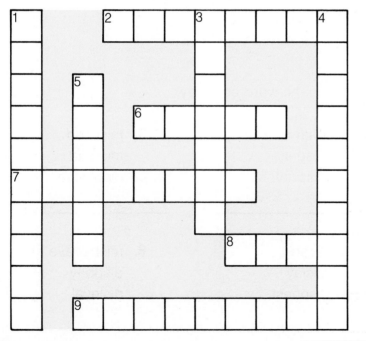

Across

2. wasn't fond of
6. understands written words
7. in a truthful manner
8. puts down
9. joined two things together

Down

1. acted badly
3. in a faithful manner
4. made someone unhappy
5. writes the letters of the alphabet

misspell misunderstand misbehave mislead misprint mislay misread misused disobey disarm dislike dishonest displease disloyal disconnect

New Words
orderly
trust
treat
conduct
informed
quoted
obedient

Reach Out for New Words

A Use the code to find the **mis** or **dis** form of each word.
Each number stands for one letter of the alphabet.
Decode each word and write it.

j	q	f	m	a	i	s	c	g	r	x	b	z	h	u	p	d	k	o	y	t	e	l	w	v	n
1	2	3	4	5	6	7	8	9	10	11	12	13	14	15	16	17	18	19	20	21	22	23	24	25	26

1. __ __ __ __ __ __ __ __   _____
   4 6 7 21 10 22 5 21

2. __ __ __ __ __ __ __ __   _____
   17 6 7 21 10 15 7 21

3. __ __ __ __ __ __ __ __ __ __   _____
   17 6 7 19 10 17 22 10 23 20

4. __ __ __ __ __ __ __ __ __ __ __   _____
   17 6 7 19 12 22 17 6 22 26 21

5. __ __ __ __ __ __ __ __ __ __   _____
   4 6 7 8 19 26 17 15 8 21

6. __ __ __ __ __ __ __ __ __   _____
   4 6 7 2 15 19 21 22 17

7. __ __ __ __ __ __ __ __ __ __ __   _____
   4 6 7 6 26 3 19 10 4 22 17

B Write the new **mis** and **dis** words in alphabetical order. Then find a word or phrase with the same meaning in the sentence.

1. _____ Bill enrolled his puppy in dog training class because his puppy was refusing to do as told.

2. _____ Jill couldn't find her notebook in her messy desk.

3. _____ Do you doubt the person who borrowed money from you?

4. _____ Ann's bad behavior surprised everyone.

5. _____ Lee gave the wrong facts to Ted about the class picnic.

6. _____ The reporter repeated incorrectly the words of the mayor.

7. _____ If you don't hurt this watch, it should last ten years.

teacher	teacher's
student	student's
coach	coach's
principal	principal's
captain	captain's
pilot	pilot's
dentist	dentist's
clerk	clerk's
waiter	waiter's
chef	chef's
hawk	hawk's
tiger	tiger's
spider	spider's
elephant	elephant's
camel	camel's

The **possessive form** of a noun shows ownership or possession.

1. What was added to each singular noun in the first column to make the possessive form in the second column? _____
2. Was the spelling of the base word changed when **'s** was added? _____

Make the possessive form of a singular noun by adding **'s**.
Do not change the spelling of the base word when you add **'s**.

tail of the tiger = the tiger's tail

Practice the Words

A Rewrite each phrase. Use the possessive form of the underlined word.

1. the paws of the <u>tiger</u>   *the tiger's paws*
2. the tray of the <u>waiter</u>   _____
3. the airplane of the <u>pilot</u>   _____
4. the chair of the <u>dentist</u>   _____
5. the eyelashes of the <u>camel</u>   _____
6. the office of the <u>principal</u>   _____
7. the cash register of the <u>clerk</u>   _____
8. the legs of the <u>spider</u>   _____
9. the wings of the <u>hawk</u>   _____
10. the recipe of the <u>chef</u>   _____
11. the pencil of the <u>student</u>   _____
12. the uniform of the <u>captain</u>   _____

B Complete each phrase with a possessive spelling word. Write each word only once.

1. _____ feathers
2. _____ homework
3. _____ web
4. _____ hump
5. _____ school
6. _____ class

7. _____ striped fur
8. _____ parachute
9. _____ trunk
10. _____ football team
11. _____ ship
12. _____ drill

Proofreading

C Proofread these sentences. Cross out each misspelled word. Write the word correctly.

1. He asked for the clerks's help in choosing his teache'rs gift.

   _____

2. A tiger's paws are smaller than an elephants feet.

   _____

3. The waiters's tray can hold six pieces of the chefs fresh pie.

   _____

4. The principals's speech was about bicycle safety.

   _____

5. Our coachs' advice was the same as our team captain's.

   _____

Build Word Power

Other singular words can also show possession.

    my   mine   your   yours   her   hers   his   its

These words are called **possessive pronouns**.
Possessive pronouns do <u>not</u> have an apostrophe.
Possessive pronouns can be used in place of possessive nouns.

    The spider is spinning *the spider's* web.
    The spider is spinning *its* web.

Find the possessive noun in each sentence. A possessive pronoun could take its place. Write the possessive pronoun.

1. The pilot, Fred Estrada, buckled the pilot's safety belt. _____

2. The camel can carry a load on the camel's back. _____

3. Kathy said to the coach, "I think this ball is the coach's." _____

4. The student said, "That book is the student's." _____

5. Our teacher, Ms. Jones, let us borrow the teacher's book. _____

6. Mr. Jackson said to the chef, "May I have the chef's secret recipe?" _____

teacher's	principal's	dentist's	chef's	spider's
student's	captain's	clerk's	hawk's	elephant's
coach's	pilot's	waiter's	tiger's	camel's

New Words

treasurer	squirrel
artist	gymnast
secretary	president
reporter	

Reach Out for New Words

A Write the possessive forms of the new words in alphabetical order. Then write a phrase with each one. The first one is done to show you.

1. *artist's*   *the artist's canvas*

2. _____   _____

3. _____   _____

4. _____   _____

5. _____   _____

6. _____   _____

7. _____   _____

Writing

B Rewrite each sentence, using the possessive form of the underlined word.

1. This notebook belongs to the <u>reporter</u>.

    _____

2. Nuts are the favorite food of the <u>squirrel</u>.

    _____

3. The trophy belongs to the <u>gymnast</u>.

    _____

4. This painting is the best work of the <u>artist</u>.

    _____

5. The typewriter of the <u>secretary</u> is broken.

    _____

6. Tim is the campaign manager of the class <u>president</u>.

    _____

7. Keeping track of money is the job of the <u>treasurer</u>.

    _____

Possessive form of plural nouns

farmers	farmer<u>s</u>'
doctors	doctor<u>s</u>'
nurses	nurse<u>s</u>'
sailors	sailor<u>s</u>'
ladies	ladie<u>s</u>'
plants	plant<u>s</u>'
animals	animal<u>s</u>'
horses	horse<u>s</u>'
mountains	mountain<u>s</u>'
trains	train<u>s</u>'
teams	team<u>s</u>'
families	familie<u>s</u>'
men	men<u>'s</u>
women	women<u>'s</u>
children	children<u>'s</u>

1. The words in the first column are plural nouns.

   How many end with **s**? _____

   How many do not end with **s**? _____

2. The words in the last column are the possessive forms of the plural nouns.

   What was added to the nouns that end with **s**? ___

   What was added to the nouns that do <u>not</u> end with **s**? ___

   When a plural noun ends with **s**, add only an apostrophe
      to make the possessive form.
   When a plural noun does not end with **s**, add **'s** to make the possessive form.
      crops that belong to the farmers = the farmers' crops
      toys that belong to the children = the children's toys

134

Practice the Words

A Use each clue to find a spelling word that fits in the puzzle. Remember to count a space for the apostrophe.

Across

2. belongs to the children
6. belongs to the families
10. of the mountains
12. belongs to the men
13. of the horses
14. belongs to the nurses
15. belongs to the women

Down

1. belongs to the teams
3. belongs to the farmers
4. of the plants
5. of the trains
7. belongs to the sailors
8. belongs to the doctors
9. of the animals
11. belongs to the ladies

B Write the possessive form of the underlined word.

1. friends of the <u>children</u>   _____

2. umbrellas of the <u>men</u>   _____

3. uniforms of the <u>sailors</u>   _____

4. luggage of the <u>ladies</u>   _____

5. engines of the <u>trains</u>   _____

6. hats of the <u>women</u>   _____

C Below are names of owners and the things they own. Write a phrase with each pair of words. Use the possessive form of each underlined word.

Thing	Owner	Possessive Phrase
1. office	doctors	_____
2. uniforms	teams	_____
3. land	farmers	_____
4. houses	families	_____
5. leaves	plants	_____
6. peaks	mountains	_____
7. caps	nurses	_____
8. fur	animals	_____
9. hoofs	horses	_____

Build Word Power

Possessive pronouns can also show possession.
    our   ours   your   yours   their   theirs

Possessive pronouns do not have an apostrophe.
Possessive pronouns can be used in place of possessive nouns.

    The doctors opened *the doctors'* new office.
    The doctors opened *their* new office.

Find the possessive noun in each sentence. A possessive pronoun could take its place. Write the possessive pronoun.

1. The sailors are docking the sailors' ship. _____

2. The police officer said to the men, "Is this car the men's?" _____

3. The children told me that those toys are not the children's. _____

4. Mr. McDonald said, "The other farmers and I are worried that insects will destroy the farmers' crops." _____

5. The doctors said, "This new office is the doctors'." _____

6. Karen said to the horses, "I'll bring the horses' food soon." _____

farmers'   sailors'   animals'   trains'   men's

doctors'   ladies'   horses'   teams'   women's

nurses'   plants'   mountains'   families'   children's

New Words	
carpenter	astronaut
company	hotel
officer	scientist
workman	

Reach Out for New Words

A Write your new words in alphabetical order on this chart. Follow the directions at the top of each column.

Singular Form	Plural Form	Possessive Form of the Plural
astronaut	*astronauts*	*astronauts'*

B Rewrite each phrase using the possessive form of the underlined word.

1. saws of the <u>carpenters</u>   _____

2. tools of the <u>workmen</u>   _____

3. guests of the <u>hotels</u>   _____

4. spacesuits of the <u>astronauts</u>   _____

5. microscopes of the <u>scientists</u>   _____

6. offices of the <u>companies</u>   _____

7. uniforms of the <u>officers</u>   _____

table
ankle
tickle
candle
purple
turtle
simple
handle
couple
pickle
people
marble
double
buckle
trouble

1. What are the last two letters of each word? _____

2. Is the letter before **le** a vowel or a consonant? _____

Many words end with a **consonant** + **le**.

138

Practice the Words

A Use each riddle to find a spelling word. Write the word.

1. a part of the leg; shaped like ⬜⬜⬜⬜ _____

2. a piece of furniture; has five letters _____

3. a stick of wax; rhymes with **handle** _____

4. synonym for **pair;** shaped like ⬜⬜⬜⬜⬜ _____

5. worry; has seven letters _____

6. part of a belt; rhymes with **chuckle** _____

7. a color; shaped like ⬜⬜⬜⬜ _____

8. twice as much; rhymes with **trouble** _____

9. humans; rhymes with **steeple** _____

10. an animal; shaped like ⬜⬜⬜⬜⬜ _____

11. flavored with dill; shaped like ⬜⬜⬜⬜ _____

12. synonym for **easy;** rhymes with **dimple** _____

13. it makes you laugh; shaped like ⬜⬜⬜ _____

14. part of a cup; rhymes with **sandal** _____

B Answer each question with spelling words. You will use some words more than once.

1. Which words end with **ckle**?

_____

2. Which words end with **ple**?

_____

3. Which words end with **ble**?

_____

4. Which words have the letters **an**?

_____

5. Which words have the letter **r**?

_____

Dictionary

Some words have more than one meaning, or definition, listed in the dictionary. Each definition is given a number.

ta·ble (tā′b'l) *n.* ①a piece of furniture with a flat top set on legs. ②a chart of facts and figures. definition numbers

C Complete each sentence with a word from the box. Look up each word in your spelling dictionary. Write the number of the meaning that was used in the sentence.

double   table   marble

1. Put the dishes on the _____*table*_____.   _____1_____

2. The statue is made of _____.   _____

3. The population of our town may _____ in ten years.   _____

4. I am studying the multiplication _____.   _____

5. The clear, blue _____ is Harry's favorite.   _____

6. I hope Don will _____ when it's his turn to bat.   _____

Build Word Power

Write new forms of your spelling words. Remember that your spelling words end with **silent e**.

1. tickle; **ing** form   _____*tickling*_____
2. turtle; plural   _____
3. marble; plural   _____
4. table; **ful** form   _____
5. buckle; **ing** form   _____
6. couple; plural   _____
7. simple; **er** form   _____
8. handle; **er** form   _____
9. double; **ed** form   _____
10. ankle; plural   _____
11. trouble; **ed** form   _____
12. simple; **est** form   _____
13. candle; plural   _____
14. pickle; **ing** form   _____

table	candle	simple	pickle	double
ankle	purple	handle	people	buckle
tickle	turtle	couple	marble	trouble

Reach Out for New Words

A Find the correct path through this maze. Words that end with a **consonant + le** are on the correct path. Write the eight words that are on the correct path.

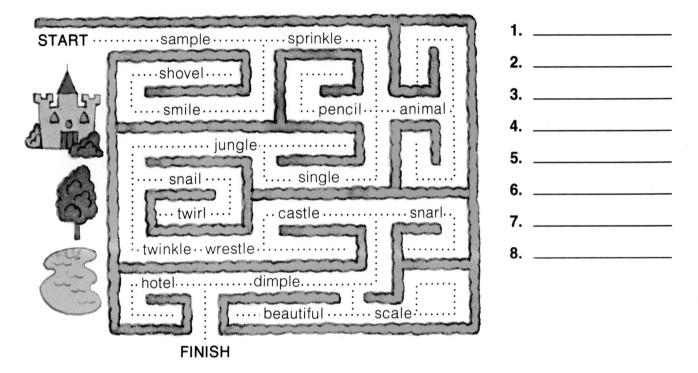

START · · · · · · sample · · · · · · · sprinkle · · · · ·

· · · · shovel · · · · ·

· · · · smile · · · · · · · · pencil · · · animal ·

· · · · jungle · · · ·

· · · snail · · · · · · · single · · · · ·

· · · twirl · · · · castle · · · · · · · · · snarl · ·

· · twinkle · · wrestle · · · · · · · ·

· · hotel · · · · · · · · · dimple · · · · · · · · ·

· · · · · · beautiful · · · · · scale ·

FINISH

1. _____
2. _____
3. _____
4. _____
5. _____
6. _____
7. _____
8. _____

B Write four silly sentences using two or more **consonant + le** words in each sentence. Use all your new **consonant + le** words. You may add endings to the words if you wish. You may also use base list words. Circle the **consonant + le** words in each sentence. An example is done to show you.

1. _My pet turtle sampled the pickle._

2. _____

_____

3. _____

_____

4. _____

_____

5. _____

_____

141

nation
station
lotion
action
fraction
question
caution
section
motion
direction
vacation
addition
invention
attention
subtraction

What are the last four letters of each word? _____

Many words end with the letters **tion**.

142

Practice the Words

A Use each clue to find a spelling word that fits in the puzzle. Some of the letters have been given to help you.

1. a place to meet a train

2. North, South, East, or West

3. hand cream

4. a new gadget

5. subtracting one number from another

6. a country

7. an act

8. keeping your mind on something

9. 1/4

10. a separate part

11. movement

12. adding numbers

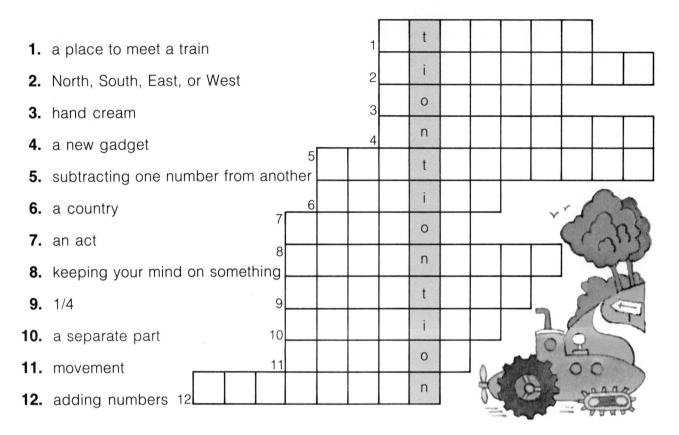

The shaded column reads vertically: t, i, o, n, t, i, o, n, t, i, o, n

B Add the missing vowels to complete each word. Then write the word.

1. s __ c t __ __ n   _____

2. __ c t __ __ n   _____

3. n __ t __ __ n   _____

4. l __ t __ __ n   _____

5. f r __ c t __ __ n   _____

6. __ n v __ n t __ __ n   _____

7. __ t t __ n t __ __ n   _____

8. d __ r __ c t __ __ n   _____

9. __ d d __ t __ __ n   _____

10. m __ t __ __ n   _____

11. s __ b t r __ c t __ __ n _____

143

Dictionary

Many words have more than one part of speech listed in the dictionary. For each part of speech there may be several definitions. These are numbered starting with **1**.

ques·tion (kwes′ chən) *n.* **1** something asked.   two noun definitions
2 a matter to be considered; problem. •*v.* to   one verb definition
ask questions of.

C Complete each sentence with a word from the box. Look up each word in your spelling dictionary. Write the part of speech and the number of the meaning that was used in the sentence.

    question   station   vacation   caution

		Part of Speech	Meaning
1. Our teacher will ___*station*___ a monitor here.		*v*	
2. Do you have a _____ about this lesson?		___	___
3. Please _____ Jill about the broken step.		___	
4. I have three days of _____ coming soon.		___	
5. The Bonatas will _____ in Europe.		___	
6. What is your favorite radio _____?		___	___
7. The police officer will _____ the suspect about the robbery.		___	
8. Use _____ when you climb the tree.		___	

Build Word Power

Write **concrete poems** with two or more of your spelling words. Make a shape with each word that reminds you of its meaning.

nation	action	caution	direction	invention
station	fraction	section	vacation	attention
lotion	question	motion	addition	subtraction

New Words
imagination
punctuation
instruction
multiplication
definition
suggestion
information

Reach Out for New Words

A Unscramble each group of syllables to make a word. There is one extra syllable in each group.

1. ma   ges   for   tion   in   _____

2. ti   tion   tu   ca   pli   mul   _____

3. tion   mag   ges   sug   _____

4. i   for   tion   def   ni   _____

5. struc   in   tion   par   _____

6. tu   a   ma   tion   punc   _____

7. i   tion   sug   i   mag   na   _____

Writing

B Many of the new words could be used to write a paragraph about school.

    Study the multiplication table . . .

    Use your imagination . . .

Pretend you are a teacher. On another sheet of paper, write out some instructions you might give your class. Try to use all your new words. You may use the plural form of some words if you wish.

apart + ment = apart*ment*
base + ment = base*ment*
pave + ment = pav*ement*
amuse + ment = amuse*ment*
excite + ment = excit*ement*
measure + ment = measure*ment*
improve + ment = improv*ement*

sad + ness = sad*ness*
ill + ness = ill*ness*
soft + ness = soft*ness*
kind + ness = kind*ness*
fair + ness = fair*ness*
happy + ness = happ*iness*
polite + ness = polite*ness*
crunchy + ness = crunch*iness*

What two suffixes were added to the base
words to make the words in the last column? _____ _____

The suffixes **ment** and **ness** are added to words to form nouns.

Practice the Words

A Write the spelling words that complete these sentences.

1. We live in an _____ on the third floor of this building.

2. Jake is recovering from a serious _____.

3. Everyone was satisfied with the _____ of the rules.

4. I like to feel the _____ of a kitten's fur.

5. Michele always treats animals with _____.

6. The _____ of our house flooded during the rainstorm.

7. The _____ is so hot that it burns the bottoms of your feet.

8. Bob felt great _____ when his best friend's family moved to another town.

9. Rosa's smile showed her _____ at winning the award.

10. We need an accurate _____ of the length of this room.

11. I love the _____ of a football game!

12. To Ron's _____, the funhouse mirror made him look two feet tall.

B Look at the base words on your spelling list. Look for **1 + 1 + 1**, **silent e**, and **consonant + y** words. Then complete the chart below.

	base word	ment/ness form
1 + 1 + 1		
silent e		
consonant + y		

C Unscramble each base word. Write each word. Then write its **ment** or **ness** form.

1. ceetix _____ _____

2. lil _____ _____

3. fots _____ _____

4. irfa _____ _____

5. knid _____ _____

6. praat _____ _____

7. seemura _____ _____

8. esuma _____ _____

9. pypha _____ _____

10. vripeom _____ _____

11. pletio _____ _____

12. chynurc _____ _____

Build Word Power

Writing

A **cinquain** is a poem that has five lines.

Line 1: a noun   Pavement

Line 2: two describing words that   Hard, rough
go with the noun

Line 3: three action words that   Walking, running, skipping
go with the noun

Line 4: four words giving a thought   Pathway to new places
or feeling about the noun

Line 5: another noun that goes with   Sidewalk
the first noun

Write two cinquains. The first word in each cinquain should be a spelling word.

_____   _____

_____   _____

_____   _____

_____   _____

_____   _____

apartment	amusement	improvement	softness	happiness
basement	excitement	sadness	kindness	politeness
pavement	measurement	illness	fairness	crunchiness

New Words

equip
lovely
entertain
lonely
develop
tender
gentle

Reach Out for New Words

A Find the **ment** or **ness** form of each new word in this puzzle.
Circle each word and write it.

road development entertainment all loveliness lonely ness gentle tenderness list one nessafeequipment

1. _____
2. _____
3. _____
4. _____
5. _____
6. _____
7. _____

B Each sentence will remind you of one of the new **ment** or **ness** words. Write the word that each sentence describes.

1. The steak can be easily cut with a fork.   _____

2. The woman's face was beautiful.   _____

3. Jan's friends were away for the summer.   _____

4. Greg stroked the kitten's fur.   _____

5. The band played and we danced.   _____

6. We took a tent, a stove, a hatchet, and a lantern on our camping trip.   _____

7. Fred's skill as a writer improves daily.   _____

149

28
friendly unfriendly
complete incomplete
expensive inexpensive

29
understand misunderstand
like dislike
honest dishonest

30
teacher teacher's
coach coach's
dentist dentist's

31
teams teams'
families families'
children children's

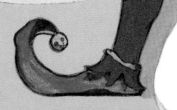

34
amuse amusement
excite excitement
kind kindness

33
question
vacation
addition

32
table
candle
double

A Complete these analogies. Write a spelling word that makes the
second pair of words go together in the same way as the first pair.

1. **expensive** is to **inexpensive**   as   **complete** is to   _____

2. **amuse** is to **amusement**   as   **excite** is to   _____

3. **pilot** is to **pilot's**   as   **dentist** is to   _____

4. **behave** is to **misbehave**   as   **understand** is to   _____

5. **coach** is to **coach's**   as   **teacher** is to   _____

6. **dislike** is to **like**   as   **dishonest** is to   _____

7. **men** is to **men's**   as   **children** is to   _____

8. **teams** is to **teams'**   as   **families** is to   _____

9. **soft** is to **softness**   as   **kind** is to   _____

10. **unlawful** is to **lawful**   as   **unfriendly** is to   _____

Proofreading

B Cross out each misspelled word. Write the word correctly.

1. The dentist's new office adition is still incomplete.

   _____

2. Both teams's uniforms are the same color.

   _____

3. I disslike people who are disonest.

   _____

4. We will visit an amusment park during our vaction.

   _____

5. I'm surprised that this record is innexpensive.

   _____

6. The unfreindly dog frightened me.

   _____

C Complete each phrase with a word from the box.

table	coach's	candle	vacation	amusement
question	double	children's	kindness	addition

1. light the _____

2. ask a _____

3. _____ and subtraction

4. the _____ game plan

5. summer _____

6. set the _____

7. the _____ toys

8. a _____ dip ice cream cone

9. _____ to animals

10. smiled in _____

Using More Review Words

A Use the directions following each base word to make another form of the word.

1. women   write the possessive form   _____

2. fold   write the **un** form   _____

3. improve   write the **ment** form   _____

4. spell   write the **mis** form   _____

5. principal   write the possessive form   _____

6. important   write the **un** form   _____

7. connect   write the **dis** form   _____

8. obey   write the **dis** form   _____

9. happy   write the **ness** form   _____

10. sad   write the **ness** form   _____

11. ladies   write the possessive form   _____

12. selfish   write the **un** form   _____

13. correct   write the **in** form   _____

14. measure   write the **ment** form   _____

15. trains   write the possessive form   _____

B Three words in each row follow the same spelling pattern. One word does not. Find that word. Be ready to tell why it does not belong.

1. action   nation   caution   simple
2. disloyal   purple   pickle   handle
3. misbehave   displease   unhurt   soft
4. captain's   plants'   camel's   pilot's
5. illness   measurement misprint   fairness
6. tiger's   sailors'   doctors'   farmers'
7. lotion   unknown   fraction   station
8. couple   double   turtle   trouble
9. men's   women's   mountains'   children's
10. pavement   basement   improvement apartment

C Complete these analogies. Write a word from the box that makes the second pair of words go together in the same way as the first pair.

basement	direction	mountains	station	incorrect
spider's	tiger's	pilot's	ankle	nation

1. **airplane** is to **airport**   as   **train** is to   _____
2. **right** is to **correct**   as   **wrong** is to   _____
3. **bus** is to **driver's**   as   **plane** is to   _____
4. **spots** are to **leopard's**   as   **stripes** are to   _____
5. **hand** is to **wrist**   as   **foot** is to   _____
6. **hive** is to **bee's**   as   **web** is to   _____
7. **low** is to **valleys**   as   **high** is to   _____
8. **above** is to **attic**   as   **below** is to   _____
9. **Boston** is to **city**   as   **United States** is to _____
10. **red** is to **color**   as   **north** is to   _____

desk	pencil	stamp	wonderful
gift	crayon	truly	envelope
neat	period	front	present
line	been	space	delivered
left	given	blank	remembered

Prewriting. Prewriting is the thinking and planning you do before you begin to write. In this lesson, you are going to plan and write a **friendly letter.**

Use Prewriting Skills

A   Answer the questions with spelling words. The words will help you think about letter writing.

1. What synonyms are things you would write to thank someone for?

   _____   _____

2. What two objects are needed to mail a letter?

   _____   _____

3. What word follows **Yours** in a letter closing? _____

4. What word tells how a letter should look? _____

5. What two words together mean an empty place on a page?

   _____   _____

6. What noun means a writing place? _____

7. What verbs could be used after **has been** or **have been** in a letter?

   _____   _____

   _____   _____

8. What word is a punctuation mark you will use? _____

B Your letter should have five main parts:

1. heading (your address and the date)
2. greeting (a simple way of saying "hello")
3. body (details you write)
4. closing (simple way of saying "goodbye")
5. signature (your handwritten name)

Use spelling words to complete these sentences. They contain other facts you need to know about writing a letter.

1. Use a ZIP code so your letter can be _____ easily.

2. Plan to write in ink, not _____ or _____ .

3. Begin the greeting on the _____ side of the page.

4. Indent the first _____ of each paragraph.

5. Write the correct address and put a stamp on the _____ of

   the _____ .

C You may plan to write a friendly letter for several reasons. You may want to share news or thank someone. You may want to give or accept an invitation. Read these phrases and decide whether they belong in a thank-you letter or an invitation. Write each phrase under the correct heading.

a wonderful present   we'll meet in front
surprise party will be given   has been delivered safely
bring a small gift   thank you for remembering

Thank–You Letter	**Invitation**
_____	_____
_____	_____
_____	_____
_____	_____
_____	_____

Now Think   Make prewriting notes for the content of your own letter to a friend. Decide what kind of letter you will write. Be sure to include enough details or information.

Writing. Use different types of language in different situations. When you write to a close friend, use informal or everyday language. When you write to adults or strangers, use more formal language. Carefully choose words that everyone will understand. Avoid slang.

Use Writing Skills

A Read the following pairs of sentences. Each pair expresses the same idea. Write the sentence in each pair that uses more formal language.

1. Hey, man, how's tricks?
   Tell me, Tom, how have you been?

   _____

2. Thank you for the wonderful game!
   Thanks for the neat game!

   _____

3. How about coming to a show next weekend?
   I truly hope you can attend a theater party next weekend.

   _____

4. I'll look forward to your delicious refreshments.
   I'll be first in line for the goodies.

   _____

5. It's so cool that you remembered my birthday.
   It was thoughtful of you to have remembered my birthday.

   _____

B Rewrite the following sentences on your own paper. Replace the underlined slang words or expressions with more formal language.

1. That meal I cooked left me feeling gross.
2. Your handmade card and envelope were really intense!
3. We signed up at the desk for the freebies.
4. I thought I remembered your number, but I drew a blank.
5. That glow-in-the-dark pencil was really neat.

Now Write Look over your prewriting notes. Use them to write a letter to a friend. Remember to include all five parts of a letter. Talk about yourself, but also ask questions. Choose language that fits the situation.

Revising. When you revise your letter, make sure that every sentence expresses a complete thought.

Use Revising and Proofreading Skills

A When you write to friends, thoughts may come faster than you can put them down on paper. You may leave out either the beginning or the ending of a sentence. For example, *the pretty gray sweater* does not tell *who* or *what happened*. Here are two ways to complete this *sentence fragment*.

I really love <u>the pretty gray sweater</u>.
<u>The pretty gray sweater</u> fits just fine.

Add words to make a complete sentence of each fragment below. Write each complete sentence on your own paper.

1. the truly useful desk set
2. his big stamp collection
3. the ZIP code on the envelope
4. a huge red crayon
5. their front door

6. your wonderful present
7. those long lines for the rides
8. the automatic pencil sharpener
9. the book with blank pages
10. our mail carrier delivered

B Proofread the following parts of a letter for mistakes in capitalization, punctuation, and spelling. Rewrite the parts correctly.

Remember
- Capitalize the names of streets, cities, and states.
- Capitalize the first word in the greeting and closing.
- Use a comma after the greeting and the closing.
- Place a comma between the city and the state, and between the date and the year.

1. dear Uncle Bill,

_____

2. yours truly

_____

3. Sincerely

_____

4. Your Freind:

_____

5. 209 Westside street
Louisville, kentucky 40205
May 20 1985

_____

_____

_____

6. Dear tracy

_____

C Revise this first draft of a friendly letter using the directions below as a guide. Then rewrite the letter correctly on your own paper.

1. Cross out a sentence with slang. Above it, write the idea in more formal language.
2. Underline a sentence fragment and add words to complete it.
3. Make up and add one missing part of the heading.
4. Circle and correct one capitalization error in the heading, one in line 2, and one in the closing.
5. Circle and correct one punctuation error in the heading, one in the greeting, and one in line 5.
6. Cross out six misspelled words. Write them correctly on the lines below.

2064 Maple Street

Summit   New jersey 07901

Dear Grandma

1   Ramember all those books I read last summer for the Library Story

2   Hour? I'm glad I did because our school will challenge Fairview school in

3   a Battle of the Books.   We will be given questions to answer about twenty

4   books. I have bin chosen captain of our team.   It'll be a real blast!   I

5   hope my mind doesn't go blank? The prizes are great! A wonderfull new

6   paperback novel.   If I win, I'll share my prezent with you when I visit this

7   summer.   By the way, can you use the stamp on this envelop for your

8   collection?

yours truely,

Randy

_____   _____   _____

_____   _____   _____

Now Revise   Read your own letter to a friend. Have you used the correct letter form? Does your language fit the situation? Are your sentences complete? Now proofread for mistakes in capitalization, punctuation, and spelling. Then write your final copy in your best handwriting.

Address an envelope and mail your letter. Your friend will enjoy seeing how you are mastering the process of writing.

Handbook

I. The Structure of Words

Syllables
Base Words
Prefixes
Suffixes
Contractions
Compound Words
Abbreviations

II. The Function of Words

Nouns
Singular Nouns
Plural Nouns
Possessive Form of Nouns
Possessive Pronouns
Verbs
Past Tense Verbs
Adjectives
Adverbs

III. The Sound of Words

Vowels
Long Vowels
Short Vowels
Consonants
Silent Letters

I. The Structure of Words means the way words are put together.

Syllables

Words are made up of parts called syllables. The dictionary shows how words are divided into syllables.

but·ter = two syllables
dress = one syllable

Base Words

Base words are words before any changes have been made.

Base word	wrap
Base word with endings added	wraps
	wrapped
	wrapping
Base word with prefix added	unwrap

Prefixes

A prefix is a syllable added to the beginning of a word to change the meaning.

I wrapped the birthday present.
(I put the paper on the present.)

I unwrapped the birthday present.
(I took the paper off the present.)

I rewrapped the birthday present.
(I put the paper back on the present.)

Suffixes

A suffix is an ending added to a word to change
the way the word is used.

soft	The pillow is <u>soft</u>.	(adjective)
soft<u>ness</u>	The baby liked the <u>softness</u> of the pillow.	(noun)
soft<u>ly</u>	Dad <u>softly</u> sang the baby to sleep.	(adverb)
soft<u>er</u>	This pillow is <u>softer</u> than that one.	(adjective)

Contractions

A contraction is made from two words. When the two words are
put together, an apostrophe takes the place of one or more letters.

we are =	we **a**re	= we're
he will =	he **wi**ll	= he'll

Compound Words

A compound word is made from two smaller words. The
spellings do not change when the words are put together.

class + room = classroom
after + noon = afternoon

Abbreviations

An abbreviation is a way to shorten a word. Abbreviations can be
made with the first few letters of a word, followed by a period.

<u>Wed</u>nesday   Wed.   <u>Aug</u>ust   Aug.   <u>in</u>ch   in.

Some abbreviations use the first and last letters of a word.

<u>D</u>octo<u>r</u>   Dr.   <u>h</u>ou<u>r</u>   hr.   <u>f</u>oo<u>t</u>   ft.

Nouns

A noun is a word that names something.

The <u>monkey</u> ate a <u>banana</u>.

The sentence has two words that are nouns.

Singular Nouns

A noun that names one thing is called a singular noun. The two nouns in this sentence are singular:

The <u>monkey</u> ate a <u>banana</u>.
(one monkey)   (one banana)

Plural Nouns

A noun that names more than one thing is a plural noun.

The <u>monkeys</u> ate a banana.
(more than one monkey)

The monkey ate two <u>bananas</u>.
(more than one banana)

Possessive Form of Nouns

The possessive form of a noun shows that something belongs to someone. Make the possessive form of a singular noun by adding **'s**.

That car belongs to my father.
That is my <u>father's</u> car.

When a plural noun ends in **s**, add only an apostrophe to make the possessive form.

Those uniforms belong to the players.
Those are the players' uniforms.

When a plural noun does <u>not</u> end in **s**, add **'s** to make the possessive form.

These toys belong to the children.
These are the children's toys.

Possessive Pronouns

A possessive pronoun takes the place of a noun in the possessive form.

My father's car = his car
The Clark's house = their house
Ashley's book = her book

A possessive pronoun is <u>not</u> spelled with an apostrophe.

Verbs

A verb is a word that tells about an action.

I walk on the beach in the summertime.
(Walk tells what I do.)

Past Tense Verbs

A verb that tells about an action that happened in the past is in the past tense.

We walked a mile to the beach.
We ran along the edge of the water.
(Walked and ran tell what we did.)

Adjectives

An adjective is a word that describes something.

> We walked on the <u>sandy</u> beach.
> (<u>Sandy</u> describes the beach.)

> We ran into the <u>cold</u> water.
> (<u>Cold</u> describes the water.)

Adverbs

An adverb is a word that tells how or how much.

> The sailor acted <u>bravely</u> during the storm.
> (<u>Bravely</u> tells how the sailor acted.)

Vowels

Five letters of the alphabet are called vowels. The vowels
are **a**, **e**, **i**, **o**, and **u**.

Long Vowels

Long vowels are easy to hear because they "say their own names."

a	**e**	**i**	**o**	**u**
nation	me	fine	no	unit

Short Vowels

Short vowels sound like the vowels in these words:

a	**e**	**i**	**o**	**u**
at	ten	is	lot	up

Consonants

The consonants are all the letters of the alphabet except
a, **e**, **i**, **o**, and **u**.

Silent Letters

Silent letters make no sound. You can see them in a word, but
you cannot hear them.

Many words have a final silent **e**.

The last letter you see in the word hope is e.
The last letter you hear in the word hope is p.

Many words begin with a silent **k** or **w**.

The first letter you see in the word knee is k.
The first letter you hear in the word knee is n.

The first letter you see in the word wrist is w.
The first letter you hear in the word wrist is r.

Some words end with a silent **b**.

climb   comb   lamb

Two letters are silent in the combination **igh**.
The letters **g** and **h** make no sound.

right   high   light

How to Find a Word

A dictionary is organized like a telephone book. It lists information in alphabetical order with guide words at the top of each page.

Guide Words

The guide words help you find the right page quickly. They tell you at a glance what section of the alphabet is included on each page. The guide word on the left tells you the first word on that page. The guide word on the right tells you the last word on that page. If the word you are looking for comes alphabetically between those two words, you are on the right page.

GUIDE WORDS

battle/bear

battle

bear

GUIDE WORDS

battle   **bear**

battle

bear

Alphabetical Order

Alphabetical order means the order of the letters in the alphabet.

Words beginning with **a** come first. **a**bout
Words beginning with **b** come next. **b**ear
Words beginning with **c** come after words beginning with **b**. **c**lass

When two words begin with the same letter, you must look at the second letter of each word to determine alphabetical order. When several of the letters are the same, you will have to look at the third or fourth letter to determine the alphabetical order.

toa**d**   The first three letters in the words <u>toad</u> and <u>toast</u>
toa**st**   are the same. The fourth letter must be used to determine alphabetical order. Since **d** comes before **s**, <u>toad</u> is alphabetized before <u>toast</u>.

Words Listed

The words listed in a dictionary are called entry words. A word is usually listed in its base form. Other forms of the word may be listed within the same entry.

Word Forms	Base Form	Entry Word
hurrying hurried	hurry	hurry
dances dancing	dance	dance

What the Dictionary Tells About a Word

A dictionary tells you much more than the spelling and meaning of a word. The information it contains about each word is called the entry. The parts of an entry are labeled and explained below.

The ENTRY WORD is printed in heavy black type. It is divided into syllables.

The RESPELLING tells you how to pronounce the word. The *Pronunciation Key* explains the respelling.

A PICTURE may be used to help you understand the meaning of the entry word.

The PART OF SPEECH is shown as an abbreviation after the pronunciation. Some words may have more than one part of speech.

The DEFINITION is the meaning of the word. If a word has more than one meaning, each meaning is given a number.

OTHER FORMS of the entry word are included in the same entry.

A STRESS MARK is placed after a syllable that gets an accent.

A sample SENTENCE can help you understand the meaning of the entry word.

sprin·kle (spring′ k'l) *v.* to scatter in drops or bits [*Sprinkle* salt on the egg.] —**sprin′ kled, sprin′ kling**

sprout (sprout) *v.* to begin to grow [Buds *sprouted* on the roses.] —**sprout′ ed, sprout′ ing**

squir·rel (skwʉr′ əl) *n.* a small, bushytailed animal that lives in trees. —*pl.* **squir′ rels**

stage (stāj) *n.* a platform or area on which plays, speeches, etc. are given. —*pl.* **stag′ es**

stair (ster) *n.* one of a series of steps going up or down. —*pl.* **stairs** a flight of steps.

stamp (stamp) *n.* a small piece of paper printed and sold by a government for sticking on a letter, etc. as proof that proper postage has been paid. —*pl.* **stamps**

star (stär) *n.* a heavenly body seen as a small light at night. —*pl.* **stars** ◆*v.* to play an important part [The actress *starred* in four movies.] —**starred, star′ ring**

stare (ster) *v.* to look steadily at [They *stared* at his Halloween costume.] —**stared, star′ ing**

sta·tion (stā′ shən) *n.* 1 a regular stopping place for a bus or train [I'll pick you up at the bus *station.*] 2 a place that sends out radio or television programs [WXYZ is a good radio *station.*] —*pl.* **sta′ tions**

Dictionary

Pronunciation Key

SYMBOL	KEY WORDS	SYMBOL	KEY WORDS	SYMBOL	KEY WORDS
a	ask, fat	u	up, cut	n	not, ton
ā	ape, date	ʉr	fur, fern	p	put, tap
ä	car, lot			r	red, dear
		ə	a in ago	s	sell, pass
e	elf, ten		e in agent	t	top, hat
er	berry, care		e in father	v	vat, have
ē	even, meet		i in unity	w	will, always
			o in collect	y	yet, yard
i	is, hit		u in focus	z	zebra, haze
ir	mirror, here				
ī	ice, fire			ch	chin, arch
		b	bed, dub	ng	ring, singer
ō	open, go	d	did, had	sh	she, dash
ô	law, horn	f	fall, off	th	thin, truth
oi	oil, point	g	get, dog	*th*	then, father
oo	look, pull	h	he, ahead	zh	s in pleasure
o͞o	ooze, tool	j	joy, jump		
yoo	unite, cure	k	kill, bake	ʹ	as in (āʹbʹl)
yo͞o	cute, few	l	let, ball		
ou	out, crowd	m	met, trim		

A heavy stress markʹ is placed after a syllable that gets a strong accent, as in **con·sid·er** (kən sidʹər).

A light stress markʹ is placed after a syllable that also gets an accent, but of a weaker kind, as in **dic·tion·ar·y** (dikʹshən erʹē).

The following abbreviations are used in your dictionary for part of speech labels. They are usually shown in dark italic type.

n.	noun	*pron.*	pronoun	*adv.*	adverb	*conj.*	conjunction
v.	verb	*adj.*	adjective	*prep.*	preposition	*interj.*	interjection

A

ac·tion (ak′ shən) *n.* the doing of something [There is not enough *action* in this movie.]

ad·di·tion (ə dish′ ən) *n.* an adding of numbers to get a total.

ad·ven·ture (əd ven′ chər) *n.* an exciting and dangerous happening [He told of his *adventures* in the jungle.] —*pl.* **ad·ven′tures**

age·less (āj′ lis) *adv.* seeming not to grow older [He spoke of the statue's *ageless* beauty.]

ag·ri·cul·ture (ag′ ri kul′ chər) *n.* farming.

a·head (ə hed′) *adv., adj.* in or to the front [Our car raced *ahead* of theirs. I am *ahead* of you in line.]

al·low (ə lou′) *v.* to let be done; permit [Swimming is not *allowed* here.] —**al·lowed′, al·low′ ing**

al·read·y (ôl red′ ē) *adv.* by or before this time [When we arrived, dinner had *already* begun.]

al·though (ôl thō′) *conj.* in spite of the fact that; even if [*Although* it's sunny, it may rain later.]

a·mount (ə mount′) *n.* **1** total [You must pay the whole *amount*.] **2** a quantity [A small *amount* of rain fell.] —*pl.* **a·mounts′**

a·muse·ment (ə myōōz′ mənt) *n.* the condition of being entertained [The clown added to our *amusement*.] —*pl.* **a·muse′ ments**

an·gry (ang′ grē) *adj.* feeling or showing anger [The *angry* man shouted at the dog.] —**an′ gri·er, an′ gri·est** —**an′ gri·ly** *adv.*

an·i·mal (an′ ə m'l) *n.* any living being that can move about by itself, has sense organs, and does not make its own food as plants do [Insects, fish, and people are kinds of *animals*.] —*pl.* **an′ i·mals**

an·kle (ang′ k'l) *n.* the joint that connects the foot and the leg. —*pl.* **an′ kles**

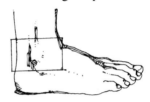

a·part·ment (ə pärt′ mənt) *n.* a room or rooms to live in [I live in a four-room *apartment*.] —*pl.* **a·part′ments**

ap·plaud (ə plôd′) *v.* to show approval by clapping [We *applauded* the wonderful concert.] —**ap·plaud′ ed, ap·plaud′ ing**

ap·point·ment (ə point′ mənt) *n.* an arrangement to meet at a certain time [I have an *appointment* with the dentist.] —*pl.* **ap·point′ ments**

ap·proach (ə prōch′) *v.* to come closer [She *approached* the dog nervously.] —**ap·proached′, ap·proach′ ing**

ar·range (ə rānj′) *v.* to put in a certain order [He *arranged* the living room furniture.] —**ar·ranged′, ar·rang′ ing**

a	fat	ir	here	ou	out	zh	leisure
ā	ape	ī	bite, fire	u	up	ng	ring
ä	car, lot	ō	go	ʉr	fur		a *in* ago
e	ten	ô	law, horn	ch	chin		e *in* agent
er	care	oi	oil	sh	she	ə =	i *in* unity
ē	even	oo	look	th	thin		o *in* collect
i	hit	ōō	tool	th	then		u *in* focus

art·ist (är′ tist) **n.** a person whose work is painting, drawing, or sculpture [The *artist* painted her portrait.] —*pl.* **art′ ists**

as·ter·oid (as′ tə roid) **n.** any of the small planets that orbit around the sun between Mars and Jupiter. —*pl.* **as′ ter·oids**

as·tro·naut (as′ trə nôt) **n.** a person trained to make rocket flights in outer space. —*pl.* **as′ tro·nauts**

at·tach (ə tach′) **v.** to fasten or join together [*Attach* the end of the rope to the boat.] —**at·tached′, at·tach′ ing**

at·ten·tion (ə ten′ shən) **n.** the act of or ability to keep one's mind on something [The principal had our *attention.*]

auc·tion (ôk′ shən) **n.** a public sale at which each thing is sold to the person offering to pay the highest price. —*pl.* **auc′tions**

au·di·ience (ô′ dē əns) **n.** a group of persons who hear and see a speaker, play, concert, etc. [The *audience* clapped wildly.] —*pl.* **au′ di·enc·es**

au·di·to·ri·um (ô′də tôr′ē əm) **n.** a room where an audience can gather. —*pl.* **au·di·to′ri·ums**

Au·gust (ô′ gəst) **n.** the eighth month of the year [The weather gets hot in *August.*]

au·thor (ô′ thər) **n.** a person who writes a book or story. —*pl.* **au′ thors**

au·to·mat·ic (ôt′ə mat′ ik) **adj.** moving or working by itself [This pencil sharpener is *automatic.*] —**au·to·mat′i·cal·ly adv.**

au·to·mo·bile (ôt′ ə mə bēl′ *or* ôt′ ə mə bēl′) **n.** a car moved by an engine. —*pl.* **au′ to·mo·biles′**

au·tumn (ôt′ əm) **n.** the season between summer and winter; fall. —*pl.* **au′ tumns**

a·void (ə void′) **v.** to keep away from [The cat *avoids* the dog.] —**a·void′ ed, a·void′ ing**

awn·ing (ô′ ning) **n.** a covering over a window or door. —*pl.* **awn′ ings**

ax (aks) **n.** a long-handled, bladed tool for chopping wood. —*pl.* **ax′ es**

B

back·ward (bak′ wərd) **adv., adj. 1** toward the back [He turned to look *backward.*] **2** in a way opposite to the usual way [Noel is Leon spelled *backward.*]

bad (bad) **adj.** not good. —**worse, worst** —**bad′ly adv.**

badge (baj) **n.** a pin or emblem that shows one belongs to a group [She wore a police *badge.*] —*pl.* **badg′ es**

bag (bag) **n.** paper, plastic, or cloth container used for holding or carrying things [Put the groceries in the *bag.*] —*pl.* **bags**

bag·ful (bag′fool) **n.** the amount that a bag will hold [Give me a *bagful* of peanuts.] —*pl.* **bag′fuls**

band·age (ban′dij) **n.** a strip of cloth used to cover a sore or wound or to bind up an injured part of the body. ♦**v.** to bind or cover with a bandage. —**band′aged, band′ag·ing**

ban·ner (ban′ ər) **n.** a piece of cloth with an emblem or words on it; a flag.

bare·ly (ber′ lē) **adv.** only just, no more than, scarcely [It is *barely* a year old.]

base·ment (bās′ mənt) *n.* the cellar or lowest room of a building.
—*pl.* **base′ ments**

bat·ter·y (bat′ ər ē) *n.* an electric cell that makes electric current. —*pl.* **bat′ ter·ies**

bawl (bôl) *v.* to cry loudly [Our baby *bawls* all day.] —**bawled, bawl′ ing**

beach (bēch) *n.* a stretch of sand at the edge of a sea or lake. —*pl.* **beach′ es**

be·cause (bi kôz′) *conj.* for the reason that [I'm late *because* I overslept.]

been (bin) past participle of the verb **be.**

be·have (bi hāv′) *v.* to act in a proper way [Try to *behave* yourself in school.]
—**be·haved′, be·hav′ ing**

be·lieve (bə lēv′) *v.* to accept as true or real [Can we *believe* that story?]
—**be·lieved′, be·liev′ ing**

bench (bench) *n.* a long, hard seat for several persons. —*pl.* **bench′ es**

be·neath (bi nēth′) *adv., adj.* underneath [The cups are on the shelf *beneath*.]
♦*prep.* below [The ground is *beneath* my feet.]

blank (blangk) *adj.* not marked or written on [I have a *blank* piece of paper.] ♦*n.* an empty space to be written in [Fill in all the *blanks*.] —*pl.* **blanks**

blaze (blāz) *n.* a bright flame or fire.
—*pl.* **blaz′ es**

bleachers (blēch′ ərz) *n. pl.* a section of seats, usually bare benches without a roof, for watching sports.

bleed (blēd) *v.* to lose blood [The wound stopped *bleeding*.] —**bled, bleed′ ing**

blot (blät) *v.* to dry by soaking up the liquid [*Blot* the spill with a paper towel.]
—**blot′ ted, blot′ ting**

blouse (blous) *n.* a shirt worn by women and children. —*pl.* **blous′ es**

blue·ber·ry (bloo′ ber′ ē) *n.* a small, round, dark-blue berry that is eaten.
—*pl.* **blue′ber′ ries**

blur (blur) *v.* to make less sharp or clear [The photograph was *blurred*.] —**blurred, blur′ ring**

boil (boil) *v.* to heat liquid until it bubbles [*Boil* the soup for five minutes.] —**boiled, boil′ ing**

bone·less (bōn′ lis) *adj.* having no bones.

boss (bôs) *n.* a person who is in charge of workers. —*pl.* **boss′ es**

boul·der (bōl′ dər) *n.* a large rock made round and smooth by weather and water.
—*pl.* **boul′ ders**

bounce (bouns) *v.* to hit against a surface so as to spring back [She *bounced* the ball against the wall.] —**bounced, bounc′ ing**

branch (branch) *n.* part of a tree growing from the trunk or a limb. —*pl.* **branch′ es**

brand (brand) *n.* **1** a mark burned on the skin with a hot iron. [*Brands* were put on cattle to show who owned them.] **2** a mark or name put on the goods of a particular company; trademark. **3** a particular kind or make [This is a new *brand* of toothpaste.]

brave (brāv) *adj.* not afraid; full of courage.
—**brav′ er, brav′ est** —**brave′ ly** *adv.*

bread (bred) *n.* a common food baked from a dough. —*pl.* **breads**

a	fat	ir	here	ou	out	zh	leisure
ā	ape	ī	bite, fire	u	up	ng	ring
ä	car, lot	ō	go	ʉr	fur		a *in* ago
e	ten	ô	law, horn	ch	chin		e *in* agent
er	care	oi	oil	sh	she		ə = i *in* unity
ē	even	oo	look	th	thin		o *in* collect
i	hit	o͞o	tool	th	then		u *in* focus

break (brāk) *v.* to come or make come apart by force; split or crack into pieces [Don't *break* that delicate vase.] —**broke, bro′ ken, break′ ing**

breathe (brē*th*) *v.* to take air into the lungs and let it out. —**breathed, breath′ ing**

breeze (brēz) *n.* a light and gentle wind. —*pl.* **breez′ es**

bridge (brij) *n.* something built over a river, railroad, etc. to serve as a path across. —*pl.* **bridg′ es**

brief (brēf) *adj.* not lasting long [We made a *brief* visit.] —**brief′ er, brief′ est** —**brief′ ly** *adv.*

bring (bring) *v.* to carry to the place where the speaker will be [*Bring* it to my house tomorrow.] —**brought, bring′ ing**

broil (broil) *v.* to cook close to a flame or high heat [You can *broil* a steak in this oven.] —**broiled, broil′ ing**

buck·et (buk′it) *n.* a round container with a flat bottom and a curved handle. —*pl.* **buck′ ets**

buck·le (buk′ ′l) *n.* a clasp on one end of a belt or strap for fastening the other end in place. —*pl.* **buck′ les**

bud (bud) *n.* a small swelling on a plant, from which a shoot, flower, or leaves will grow. —*pl.* **buds** ♦*v.* to begin to show buds. —**bud′ded, bud′ ding**

bur·y (ber′ ē) *v.* to cover up, to hide [He *buried* the candy in his pocket.] —**bur′ ied, bur′ y·ing**

bush (boosh) *n.* a plant smaller than a tree; shrub. —*pl.* **bush′ es**

busi·ness (biz′ nis) *n.* **1** the buying and selling of goods and services. **2** a store or factory [She owns a thriving candy *business*.] —*pl.* **busi′ ness·es**

bus·y (biz′ ē) *adj.* full of activity, not idle [We were *busy* all morning.] —**bus′ i·er, bus′ i·est** —**bus′ i·ly** *adv.*

buy (bī) *v.* to get by paying money [*Buy* apples at the store.] —**bought, buy′ ing**

C

cab·in (kab′ in) *n.* **1** a small house built in a simple way, usually of wood. **2** a space on a ship or an airplane where passengers ride. —*pl.* **cab′ ins**

cam·el (kam′ ′l) *n.* a large animal with a humped back that lives in Asian and North African deserts. —*pl.* **cam′ els**

can (kan) *a helping verb used with other verbs meaning:* to know how or be able to [The baby *can* walk.] —**could**

ca·nar·y (kə ner′ ē) *n.* a small, yellow songbird. —*pl.* **ca·nar′ ies**

can·dle (kan′ d′l) *n.* a stick of wax with a wick that gives light when burned. —*pl.* **can′ dles**

cap·tain (kap′ t′n) *n.* a chief or leader of a group or activity [They saluted the *captain*.] —*pl.* **cap′ tains**

cap·ture (kap′ chər) *v.* to catch and hold by force [He *captured* the runaway dog.] —**cap′ tured, cap′ tur·ing**

care·ful (ker′ fəl) *adj.* taking care to avoid having mistakes or accidents [Be *careful* when you cross streets.] —**care′ ful·ly** *adv.*

car·pen·ter (kär′ pən tər) *n.* a worker who builds and repairs wooden things. —*pl.* **car′ pen·ters**

case (kās) **n.** a single example or happening [I had a bad *case* of the measles.] **2** a container for holding something [Be careful with the violin *case*.] —*pl.* **cas′ es**

cash·ier (ka shir′) **n.** a person who handles money in a bank, store, or restaurant.

cas·tle (kas′ ′l) **n.** a large building where a king or noble lived in the Middle Ages. —*pl.* **cas′ tles**

catch (kach) **v.** to take hold of; capture [The police *caught* the thief.] **2** to stop by grasping with the hands [Can you *catch* that football?] —**caught, catch′ ing**

cau·tion (kô′ shən) **n.** being careful to avoid danger or mistakes [Use *caution* in crossing streets.] ♦**v.** to warn [The sign *cautioned* us to slow down.] —**cau′ tioned, cau′ tion·ing**

ceil·ing (sēl′ ing) **n.** the top part of a room. —*pl.* **ceil′ ings**

cent (sent) **n.** a coin worth one-100th part of a dollar; penny. —*pl.* **cents**

ce·re·al (sir′ ē əl) **n.** **1** any grass that bears seeds used for food [Rice, wheat, and oats are *cereals*.] **2** food made from these seeds, especially breakfast food, as oatmeal or cornflakes. —*pl.* **ce′ re·als**

chal·lenge (chal′ ənj) **v.** to call to take part in a contest; dare [He *challenged* him to a duel.] —**chal′ lenged, chal′ leng·ing** ♦**n.** a hard task [Climbing the mountain was a *challenge*.] —*pl.* **chal′ leng·es**

chance (chans) **n.** **1** happening of events by accident [They left the future to *chance*.] **2** opportunity [This is your *chance* to succeed.] **3** a risk [Take a *chance* on winning.] —*pl.* **chanc′ es**

change·less (chānj′ lis) **adj.** remaining the same [Some people say this town is *changeless*.]

chat (chat) **v.** to talk in an easy way [The neighbors *chatted* every day.] —**chat′ ted, chat′ ting**

cheap (chēp) **adj.** **1** low in price [Vegetables are *cheaper* in summer than in winter.] **2** of low value or of poor quality [*Cheap* shoes may wear out quickly.] —**cheap′ er, cheap′ est**

chef (shef) **n.** a head cook in a restaurant. —*pl.* **chefs**

chief (chēf) **n.** the leader of a group [The police *chief* gave orders to the officers.] —*pl.* **chiefs**

child (chīld) **n.** a young boy or girl. —*pl.* **chil′ dren**

chim·ney (chim′ nē) **n.** a pipe going through a roof to carry smoke away [A wind blew over our *chimney*.] —*pl.* **chim′ neys**

choice (chois) **n.** a person or thing chosen [Smith is my *choice* for mayor.] —*pl.* **choic′ es**

cir·cus (sur′ kəs) **n.** a traveling show with clowns, trained animals, and acrobats. —*pl.* **cir′ cus·es**

a	fat	ir	here	ou	out	zh	leisure
ā	ape	ī	bite, fire	u	up	ng	ring
ä	car, lot	ō	go	ur	fur		a *in* ago
e	ten	ô	law, horn	ch	chin		e *in* agent
er	care	oi	oil	sh	she	ə	= i *in* unity
ē	even	oo	look	th	thin		o *in* collect
i	hit	ōo	tool	th	then		u *in* focus

clap (klap) **v.** to strike the hands together, as in applauding [We *clapped* when our side won.] —**clapped, clap′ ping**

claw (klô) **n.** a sharp nail on the foot of an animal or bird [The cat broke its *claw*.] —*pl.* **claws**

clerk (klʉrk) **n.** **1** an office worker who keeps records. **2** a salesperson in a store. —*pl.* **clerks**

clip (klip) **n.** anything that holds things together [I prefer a paper *clip* to a staple.] —*pl.* **clips** ◆*v.* to cut. —**clipped, clip′ ping**

clip·ping (klip′ ing) **n.** a piece cut off or out of something [Cut a *clipping* from a plant.] —*pl.* **clip′ pings**

close (klōs) **adj.** **1** with not much space between; near. **2** thorough or careful [Pay *close* attention.] —**clos′ er, clos′ est** —**close′ ly** *adv.*

clown (kloun) **n.** a person who entertains by doing comical tricks. —*pl.* **clowns**

coach (kōch) **n.** a person who trains students, athletes, singers, etc. [The swimming *coach* taught diving.] —*pl.* **coach′ es**

coil (koil) **v.** to wind around in circles or in a spiral [The sailors *coiled* the ropes.] —**coiled, coil′ ing**

coin (koin) **n.** a piece of metal money. —*pl.* **coins**

cole·slaw (kōl′ slô) **n.** a salad made of shredded raw cabbage.

com·pa·ny (kum′ pə nē) **n.** a group of people joined together in work or activity [He works for a large *company*.] —*pl.* **com′ pa·nies**

com·plete (kəm plēt′) **adj.** having no parts missing; full; whole [Her coin collection is *complete*.] —**com·plete′ ly** *adv.*

con·ceit′ ed (kən sēt′ əd) **adj.** having a high opinion of oneself.

couch (kouch) **n.** a piece of furniture for sitting or lying on; sofa. —*pl.* **couch′ es**

cough (kôf) **v.** to force air from the lungs with a loud noise [The dust made him *cough*.] —**coughed, cough′ ing**

could (kood) *past tense of* **can** [Years ago you *could* buy a hamburger for five cents.]

could·n't (kood′ ′nt) could not.

count·er (koun′ tər) **n.** a long table. —*pl.* **count′ ers**

coun·try (kun′ trē) **n.** **1** land outside of cities [Let's drive out to the *country*.] **2** the whole land of a nation [The *country* of Japan is made up of islands.] —*pl.* **coun′ tries**

cou·ple (kup′ ′l) **n.** pair [I have a *couple* of bookends.]

course (kôrs) **n.** **1** a way along which something moves. **2** one of a series of studies [I took a math *course*.] —*pl.* **cours′ es**

court (kôrt) **n.** **1** an open space with buildings or walls around it. **2** a space marked out for playing some game. **3** the palace of a king or other ruler. **4** a place where law trials are held. — *pl.* **courts**

crawl (krôl) **v.** to move by dragging the body [The baby *crawled* across the room.] —**crawled, crawl′ ing**

cray·on (krā′ ən *or* krā′ än) **n.** a small stick of chalk, charcoal, or colored wax, used for drawing or writing. —*pl.* **cray′ ons**

cream (krēm) **n.** the yellowish part of milk that contains the butterfat.

crea·ture (krē′ chər) **n.** a living being. —*pl.* **crea′ tures**

crunch·y (krunch′ ē) **adj.** making a crunching sound [Celery is *crunchy*.]

—**crunch′ i·er, crunch′ i·est**
—**crunch′ i·ness** *n.*

crutch (kruch) *n.* a support used under the arm to help in walking. —*pl.* **crutch′ es**

cub (kub) *n.* the young of certain animals. —*pl.* **cubs**

cube (kyo͞ob) *n.* a solid with six square, equal sides. —*pl.* **cubes**

cul·ture (kul′ chər) *n.* way of life; civilization [The *culture* of the Aztecs is interesting.] —*pl.* **cul′ tures**

cup (kup) *n.* a small container for drinking from. —*pl.* **cups**

cup·ful (kup′ fool) *n.* as much as a cup will hold [May I have a *cupful* of flour?] —*pl.* **cup′ fuls**

curl·y (kʉr′ lē) *adj.* full of ringlets or coils [Lambs have *curly* fur.] –**curl′ i·er, curl′ i·est**

cur·tain (kʉr′ tən) *n.* a piece of cloth or other material hung at a window, in front of a stage, etc., to decorate or to shut off. —*pl.* **cur′ tains**

curve (kʉrv) *n.* a line with no straight parts. —*pl.* **curves** •*v.* to turn or bend to form a curve [The road *curves* around the mountain.] —**curved, cur′ ving**

cut (kut) *v.* to divide into parts with a knife or sharp tool [Will you *cut* the cake?] —**cut, cut′ ting**

cute (kyo͞ot) *adj.* pretty or pleasing [What a *cute* little puppy!] —**cut′ er, cut′ est** —**cute′ ly** *adv.*

cut·ter (kut′ ər) *n.* a person or thing that cuts. —*pl.* **cut′ ters**

D

damp (damp) *adj.* slightly wet, moist.

dare (der) *v.* **1** to face bravely. **2** to challenge [She *dared* me to swim across the lake.] —**dared, dar′ ing**

daugh·ter (dôt′ ər) *n.* a girl or woman as she is related to a parent. —*pl.* **daugh′ ters**

dawn (dôn) *n.* the beginning of day [We saw the sunrise at *dawn*.]

de·fense·less (di fens′ lis) *adj.* not able to protect oneself [Without the soldiers, the town was left *defenseless*.]

def·i·ni·tion (def′ ə nish′ ən) *n.* a statement that tells what a word means [Find the *definition* in the dictionary.] —*pl.* **def′ i·ni′ tions**

de·liv·er (di liv′ ər) *v.* to bring and hand over. —**de·liv′ ered, de·liv′ er·ing**

den·tist (den′ tist) *n.* a doctor who takes care of teeth. —*pl.* **den′ tists**

de·ny (di nī′) *v.* to say that something is not true [Why *deny* the truth?] —**de·nied′, de·ny′ ing**

de·par·ture (di pär′ chər) *n.* a going away. —*pl.* **de·par′ tures**

desk (desk) *n.* a piece of furniture with a smooth top on which one can write, draw, or read. —*pl.* **desks**

de·vel·op·ment (di vel′ əp mənt) *n.* **1** the act of developing. **2** a thing that is developed. —*pl.* **de·vel′ op·ments**

a	fat	ir	here	ou	out	zh	leisure
ā	ape	ī	bite, fire	u	up	ng	ring
ä	car, lot	ō	go	ʉr	fur		a *in* ago
e	ten	ô	law, horn	ch	chin		e *in* agent
er	care	oi	oil	sh	she	ə = i *in* unity
ē	even	oo	look	th	thin		o *in* collect
i	hit	o͞o	tool	th	then		u *in* focus

dim (dim) *adj.* not bright or clear; gloomy [It's too *dim* to see in here.] —**dim′ mer, dim′ mest** —**dim′ ly** *adv.*

dim·ple (dim′ p'l) *n.* a small, hollow spot. —*pl.* **dim′ ples**

dine (dīn) *v.* to eat dinner. —**dined, din′ ing**

di·rec·tion (də rek′ shən) *n.* the point toward which something faces [What *direction* are we going?] —*pl.* **di·rec′ tions**

dis·ap·point (dis ə point′) *v.* to fail to give or do what is expected [The team's poor playing *disappointed* the fans.] —**dis·ap·point′ ed, dis·ap·point′ ing**

dis·arm (dis ärm′) *v.* to take away weapons from [The police *disarmed* the robbers.] —**dis·armed′, dis·arm′ ing**

dis·con·nect (dis kə nekt′) *v.* to undo the connection of [Please *disconnect* the toaster.] —**dis·con·nect′ ed, dis·con·nect′ ing**

dis·hon·est (dis än′ ist) *adj.* not honest; lying, cheating [The *dishonest* clerk was fired.] —**dis·hon′ est·ly** *adv.*

dis·like (dis līk′) *v.* to have a feeling of not liking [I *dislike* rude people.] —**dis·liked′, dis·lik′ ing**

dis·loy·al (dis loi′ əl) *adj.* not loyal or faithful [The guard was *disloyal*.] —**dis·loy′ al·ty** *n.*

dis·o·be·di·ent (dis′ o·be′ di·ənt) *adj.* refusing to obey [The *disobedient* child ignored her father.] —**dis′ o·be′ di·ence** *n.*

dis·o·bey (dis ə bā′) *v.* to fail or refuse to obey [He *disobeyed* the rules.] —**dis·o·beyed′, dis·o·bey′ ing**

dis·or·der·ly (dis ôr′ dər lē) *adj.* untidy; messy [His bedroom is very *disorderly*.]

dis·play (dis plā′) *n.* showing exhibition [The *display* of jewelry is beautiful.] —*pl.* **dis·plays′**

dis·please (dis plēz′) *v.* to make angry; annoy [Her bad behavior *displeased* her grandmother.] —**dis·pleased′, dis·pleas′ ing**

dis·trust (dis trust′) *n.* a lack of trust; doubt; suspicion [His strange behavior caused *distrust*.] ♦*v.* to doubt [I *distrust* what she says.] —**dis·trust′ ed, dis·trust′ ing**

ditch (dich) *n.* trench [Be careful of the *ditch* along the road.] —*pl.* **ditch′ es**

diz·zy (diz′ ē) *adj.* having a spinning feeling that makes one unsteady [The merry-go-round made us *dizzy*.] —**diz′ zi·er, diz′ zi·est** —**diz′ zi·ly** *adv.*

doc·tor (däk′ tər) *n.* a person trained to heal the sick. —*pl.* **doc′ tors**

dodge (däj) *v.* to move quickly to one side so as to get out of the way [He *dodged* the charging goat.] —**dodged, dodg′ ing** —**dodg′ er** *n.*

does·n't (duz′ 'nt) does not.

dou·ble (dub′ 'l) *adj.* twice as much [Give me a *double* portion.] ♦*n.* 1 an amount that is twice as much. 2 a hit in baseball on which the batter gets to second base. —*pl.* **dou′ bles** ♦*v.* 1 to make twice as much. 2 to hit a double in baseball. —**dou′ bled, dou′ bling**

dough (dō) *n.* a mixture of flour, liquid, and other ingredients for baking into bread or pastry. —*pl.* **doughs**

drag (drag) *v.* to pull slowly along the ground [She *dragged* the sled upstairs.] —**dragged, drag′ ging**

draw (drô) *v.* to make a picture or design with a pencil or pen [Can you *draw* cartoons?] —**drew, drawn, draw′ ing**

dream (drēm) *n.* thoughts or feelings in the mind of a sleeping person [A bad *dream* woke her up.] ◆*v.* to have a dream [I *dreamed* I was in Africa.] —**dreamed, dream′ ing**

drench (drench) *v.* to make wet all over; soak [We were *drenched* by the rain.] —**drenched, drench′ ing**

drip (drip) *v.* to let drops of liquid fall [That faucet *drips*.] —**dripped, drip′ ping**

drown (droun) *v.* to die or kill by keeping under water. —**drowned, drown′ ing**

dust (dust) *n.* fine, powdery earth or other material that floats in the air and settles on surfaces. ◆*v.* to wipe the dust from [*Dust* the table with this cloth.] —**dust′ ed, dust′ ing**

du·ty (do͞ot′ ē) *n.* any of the things to be done as a part of a person's work [These are the *duties* of a secretary.] —*pl.* **du′ ties**

E

ea·ger (ē′ gər) *adj.* anxious to do or get [We are *eager* to win.] —**ea′ ger·ly** *adv.*

ear·ly (ʉr′ lē) *adj.* soon after the start [We left in the *early* afternoon.] —**ear′ li·er, ear′ li·est**

edge (ej) *n.* the part where something begins or ends; border [We walked to the *edge* of town.] —*pl.* **edg′ es**

eight (āt) *adj.* a number, one more than seven.

el·e·phant (el′ ə fənt) *n.* a huge animal with thick skin, two ivory tusks, and a trunk. —*pl.* **el′ e·phants**

emp·ty (emp′ tē) *v.* to pour out [*Empty* the water pitcher into the sink.] —**emp′ tied,**

emp′ ty·ing ◆*adj.* having nothing in it [Don't go near the *empty* house.] —**emp′ ti·er, emp′ ti·est** —**emp′ ti·ly** *adv.*

e·nough (i nuf′) *adj.* as much as needed [There is *enough* food for all.] ◆*adv.* to the right amount [Is your steak cooked *enough*?]

en·ter·tain·ment (en′ tər tān′ mənt) *n.* something that gives pleasure [Movies are his favorite type of *entertainment*.] —*pl.* **en′ ter·tain′ ments**

en·tire·ly (in tīr′ lē) *adv.* completely.

en·vel·ope (en′ və lōp) *n.* a folded paper cover in which letters are sealed for mailing. —*pl.* **en′ ve·lopes**

e·quip·ment (i kwip′ mənt) *n.* the outfit, supplies, etc., needed for some purpose [We brought all the right camping *equipment*.]

es·cape (ə skāp′) *v.* to break loose or get free [The criminals *escaped* from jail.] —**es·caped′, es·cap′ ing**

ex·change (iks chānj′) *v.* to give in return for something else; trade [We *exchanged* telephone numbers.] —**ex·changed′, ex·chang′ ing**

ex·cite·ment (ik sīt′ mənt) *n.* anything that causes strong feeling [The burning house caused great *excitement* in town.]

a	fat	ir	here	ou	out	zh	leisure
ā	ape	ī	bite, fire	u	up	ng	ring
ä	car, lot	ō	go	ʉr	fur		a *in* ago
e	ten	ô	law, horn	ch	chin		e *in* agent
er	care	oi	oil	sh	she	ə =	i *in* unity
ē	even	oo	look	th	thin		o *in* collect
i	hit	o͞o	tool	th	then		u *in* focus

eye·brow (ī′ brou) **n.** the hair growing on the curved, bony part over each eye. —*pl.* **eye′ brows**

F

fact (fakt) **n.** a thing that has actually happened or that is really true [I can't deny the *fact* that I was late.] —*pl.* **facts**

fac·to·ry (fak′ tə rē) **n.** a building where goods are made [He works at a furniture *factory*.] —*pl.* **fac′ to·ries**

fair·ness (fer′ nis) **n.** justness and honesty [That judge is famous for his *fairness*.]

fam·i·ly (fam′ ə lē) **n.** a group made up of one or two parents and their children [Everyone in his *family* wears glasses.] —*pl.* **fam′ i·lies**

fan·cy (fan′ sē) **adj.** of better quality than the usual [She wore her *fancy* dress to the party.] —**fan′ ci·er, fan′ ci·est**

farm·er (fär′ mər) **n.** a person who owns or works on a farm. —*pl.* **farm′ ers**

fau·cet (fô′ sit) **n.** a device that controls the flow of liquid [Turn on the water *faucet*.] —*pl.* **fau′ cets**

fault (fôlt) **n.** blame; responsibility [It's not my *fault* we're late.] —*pl.* **faults**

fawn (fôn) **n.** a young deer. —*pl.* **fawns**

feath·er (feth′ ər) **n.** any of the parts that grow out of the skin of birds. —*pl.* **feath′ ers**

fea·ture (fē′ chər) **n.** any part of the face [That girl has lovely *features*.] —*pl.* **fea′ tures**

fence (fens) **n.** a railing or wall put around a field or yard. —*pl.* **fenc′ es**

fetch (fech) **v.** to go after and bring back [The dog *fetched* my slippers.] —**fetched, fetch′ ing**

field (fēld) **n.** a piece of land having a special use, especially for growing [The farmer plowed the *field*.] —*pl.* **fields**

fierce (firs) **adj.** wild; violent [The *fierce* dog scared the campers.] —**fierc′ er, fierc′ est** —**fierce′ ly adv.**

fight (fīt) **v.** to use fists or force in trying to beat someone or something; battle [Don't *fight* with your brother.] —**fought, fight′ ing**

fit (fit) **v.** to be the right size or shape for [Does this coat *fit* you?] —**fit′ ted, fit′ ting** ◆**n.** the way something fits [This coat is a tight *fit*.]

fit·ness (fit′ nis) **n.** the state of being in good physical condition [A good diet is important to physical *fitness*.]

fix·ture (fiks′ chər) **n.** any of the fittings fastened to a building [We must fix the light *fixture*.] —*pl.* **fix′ tures**

flaw (flô) **n.** a break or scratch, that spoils something [Most diamonds have a *flaw*.] —*pl.* **flaws**

flow·er (flou′ ər) **n.** the part of a plant that bears the seed and has brightly colored petals. —*pl.* **flow′ ers**

flur·ry (flur′ ē) **n.** a sudden, light fall of rain or snow. —*pl.* **flur′ ries**

foil (foil) **n.** a very thin sheet of metal [Wrap it in aluminum *foil*.] —*pl.* **foils**

force·ful (fôrs′ fəl) **adj.** strong; powerful [She gave a *forceful* speech.] —**force′ ful·ly adv.**

for·ev·er (fər ev′ ər) **adv.** for all time; without ever coming to an end [No person lives *forever*.]

for·ward (fôr′ wərd) *adj.; adv.* at or toward the front. ◆*n.* a player in a front position, as in basketball or hockey. —*pl.* **for′ wards**

frac·tion (frak′ shən) *n.* a quantity less than a whole; one or more equal parts of a whole. —*pl.* **frac′ tions**

frac· ture (frak′ chər) *v.* to break or crack [He *fractured* his arm.] —**frac′ tured, frac′ tur·ing,** ◆*n.* a break or crack. —*pl.* **frac′ tures**

frame (frām) *v.* to put a border around [*Frame* the picture.] —**framed, fram′ ing**

freeze (frēz) *v.* to harden into ice; make or become solid because of cold [Water *freezes* at 0°C.] —**froze, fro′ zen, freez′ ing**

freight (frāt) *n.* a load of goods shipped [They loaded the *freight* on the train.] —*pl.* **freights**

friend·ly (frend′ lē) *adj.* showing good feelings; ready to be a friend [The big dog was not *friendly*.] —**friend′ li·er, friend′ li·est**

fringe (frinj) *n.* loose or bunches of threads used for decoration [The curtains have a *fringe*.] —*pl.* **fring′ es** ◆*adj.* additional [The company offered many *fringe* benefits.]

front (frunt) *n.* **1** the part that faces forward. **2** the beginning [That chapter is toward the *front* of the book.] —*pl.* **fronts**

fron·tier (frun tir′) *n.* the part of a country next to a wilderness [Alaska is our last *frontier*.] —*pl.* **fron·tiers′**

fudge (fuj) *n.* a soft candy.

fur·ni·ture (fʉr′ ni chər) *n.* the things needed for living in a house.

fu·ture (fyōō′ chər) *n.* the time that is to come [We'll buy a car sometime in the *future*.]

G

ga·rage (gə räzh′ *or* gə räj′) *n.* a closed place where automobiles are kept. —*pl.* **ga·rag′ es**

gen·tle (jent′ ′l) *adj.* **1** not rough [a *gentle* scolding]. **2** easy to handle [a *gentle* horse]. —**gen′ tler, gen′ tlest** —**gen′ tle·ness** *n.*

get (get) *v.* **1** to become the owner of by receiving, buying, etc. **2** to arrive at, reach [They *got* home early.] **3** to go and bring [*Get* your books.] —**got, got′ ten, get′ ting**

gift (gift) *n.* something given; a present. —*pl.* **gifts**

give (giv) *v.* to pass or hand over to another; to supply. —**gave, giv′ en; giv′ ing**

glad (glad) *adj.* feeling joy; happy [I'm *glad* to be here.] —**glad′ der, glad′ dest** —**glad′ ly** *adv.* —**glad′ ness** *n.*

gloom·y (glōōm′ ē) *adj.* **1** dark or dim. **2** having or giving a feeling of deep sadness [He told a *gloomy story*.] —**gloom′ i·er, gloom′ i·est**

go (gō) *v.* to move along from one point to another [Time *goes* fast.] —**went, gone, go′ ing**

a	fat	**ir**	here	**ou**	out	**zh**	leisure
ā	ape	**ī**	bite, fire	**u**	up	**ng**	ring
ä	car, lot	**ō**	go	**ʉr**	fur		a *in* ago
e	ten	**ô**	law, horn	**ch**	chin		e *in* agent
er	care	**oi**	oil	**sh**	she	**ə** = i *in* unity
ē	even	**oo**	look	**th**	thin		o *in* collect
i	hit	**ōō**	tool	**th**	then		u *in* focus

goal (gōl) *n.* **1** the place at which a race is ended or at which a point is scored in certain games. **2** aim or purpose [His *goal* was to become a nurse.] —*pl.* **goals**

grab (grab) *v.* to snatch suddenly [The toddler *grabbed* the baby's toy.] —**grabbed, grab′ bing**

grace·ful (grās′ fəl) *adj.* having a beauty of form or movement [Ballet dancers are very *graceful*.] —**grace′ ful·ly** *adv.*

great (grāt) *adj.* fine or excellent [He gave a *great* party.] —**great′ ly** *adv.*

greed·y (grēd′ ē) *adj.* wanting or taking all that one can get with no thought of others' needs [The *greedy* girl ate all the cookies.] —**greed′ i·er, greed′ i·est** —**greed′ i·ly** *adv.*

grim (grim) *adj.* looking stern or harsh [The judge's face was *grim*.] —**grim′ mer, grim′ mest** —**grim′ ly** *adv.*

grip (grip) *v.* to grasp and hold fast. —**gripped, grip′ ping** ◆*n.* a grasping.

gro·cer·y (grō′ sər ē) *n.* **1** a store selling food and household supplies. **2 groceries,** *pl.* the goods sold by a grocer. —*pl.* **gro′ cer·ies**

growl (groul) *v.* to make a rumbling sound in the throat [Our dog *growled* at him.] —**growled, growl′ ing**

guide (gīd) *v.* to show the way; lead [Can you *guide* me through the museum?] —**guid′ ed, guid′ ing**

gym·nast (jim′ nast) *n.* a person trained in doing athletic exercises. —*pl.* **gym′ nasts**

H

han·dle (han′ d'l) *n.* the part by which a tool, door, cup, etc. can be held with the hand. —*pl.* **han′ dles**

hap·pi·ness (hap′ ē nis) *n.* a feeling of joy; gladness [Their laughter showed their *happiness*.]

has·n't (haz′ 'nt) has not.

haunt (hônt) *v.* to visit often [Ghosts are supposed to *haunt* old houses.] —**haunt′ ed, haunt′ ing**

have·n't (hav′ 'nt) have not.

hawk (hôk) *n.* a large bird with a strong, hooked beak and claws. —*pl.* **hawks**

ha·zy (hā′ zē) *adj.* misty or smoky [It was a *hazy* autumn day.] —**ha′ zi·er, ha′ zi·est**

head (hed) *n.* the top part of the body containing the brain and face. —*pl.* **heads**

health·y (hel′ thē) *adj.* having good health. —**health′ i·er, health′ i·est**

hedge (hej) *n.* a row of shrubs planted close together [She got scratched jumping over the *hedge*.] —*pl.* **hedg′ es**

hem (hem) *v.* to fold back the edge and sew down [Ron *hemmed* his new jeans.] —**hemmed, hem′ ming**

here's (hirz) here is.

high·way (hī′ wā) *n.* a main road. —*pl.* **high′ ways**

hinge (hinj) *n.* a joint on which a door, lid, etc. swings open and shut. —*pl.* **hin′ ges**

hoist (hoist) *v.* to lift or pull up [*Hoist* the statue into place.] —**hoist′ ed, hoist′ ing**

hol·i·day (häl′ ə dā) *n.* a day set aside to celebrate some event. —*pl.* **hol′ i·days**

home·less (hōm′ lis) *adj.* not having a home or place to live [She found a *homeless* puppy.]

hop (häp) *v.* to move by short jumps, as a bird or frog. —**hopped, hop′ ping**

hope (hōp) *v.* to have a feeling that what one wants and expects will happen [I *hope* that you win.] —**hoped, hop′ ing**

hope·ful (hōp′ fəl) *adj.* feeling or showing hope [Our team was *hopeful* about winning.] —**hope′ ful·ly** *adv.*

horse (hôrs) *n.* a large, four-legged animal with a mane and tail. —*pl.* **hors′ es**

ho·tel (hō tel′) *n.* a building where travelers may rent rooms, buy meals, etc. —*pl.* **ho·tels′**

hound (hound) *n.* a hunting dog with long, drooping ears and short hair. —*pl.* **hounds**

howl (houl) *n.* a long, wailing cry of wolves or dogs or a sound like it [The dog *howled* in pain.] —*pl.* **howls**

huge (hyōōj) *adj.* very large [Dinosaurs were *huge* creatures.] —**huge′ ly** *adv.*

I

i·cy (ī′ sē) *adj.* full of or covered with ice [Be careful of the *icy* streets.] —**i′ ci·er, i′ ci·est** —**i′ ci·ly** *adv.*

i·de·a (ī dē′ ə) *n.* something one thinks, knows, imagines; belief or thought. —*pl.* **i·de′ as**

ill·ness (il′ nis) *n.* being in poor health; sickness; disease [She took medicine for her *illness*.] —*pl.* **ill′ ness·es**

i·mag·i·na·tion (i maj′ ə nā′ shən) *n.* the power of making up ideas in the mind [In his *imagination*, he saw himself as king.] —*pl.* **i·mag′ i·na′ tions**

im·me·di·ate (i mē′ dē it) *adj.* without delay [The medicine had an *immediate* effect.] **im·me′ di·ate·ly** *adv.*

im·prove·ment (im prōōv′ mənt) *n.* a making or becoming better [Your playing shows *improvement*.] —*pl.* **im·prove′ ments**

in·com·plete (in kəm plēt′) *adj.* not complete; not whole or finished [The party would seem *incomplete* without you.] —**in·com·plete′ ly** *adv.*

in·con·sid·er·ate (in′ kən sid′ ər it) *adj.* not thoughtful of other people [Those *inconsiderate* people left their litter on the beach.] —**in′ con·sid′ er·ate·ly** *adv.*

in·cor·rect (in kə rekt′) *adj.* not correct; wrong [Your answer to the question was *incorrect*.] —**in·cor·rect′ ly** *adv.*

in·di·ges·tion (in di jes′ chən) *n.* difficulty in digesting food [The spicy meatballs gave her *indigestion*.]

in·ex·pen·sive (in′ ik spen′ siv) *adj.* not expensive; low priced [That shirt is *inexpensive*.] —**in′ ex·pen′ sive·ly** *adv.*

in·for·ma·tion (in′ fər mā′ shən) *n.* something told or facts learned; news or knowledge [An encyclopedia gives *information* about many things.]

in·ju·ry (in′ jər ē) *n.* harm done to a person or thing [She got that *injury* when she fell.] —*pl.* **in′ ju·ries**

a	fat	ir	here	ou	out	zh	leisure
ā	ape	ī	bite, fire	u	up	ng	ring
ä	car, lot	ō	go	ʉr	fur		a *in* ago
e	ten	ô	law, horn	ch	chin		e *in* agent
er	care	oi	oil	sh	she	ə =	i *in* unity
ē	even	oo	look	th	thin		o *in* collect
i	hit	ōō	tool	th	then		u *in* focus

in·stead (in sted′) *adv.* in place of the other [Use milk *instead* of cream.]

in·struc·tion (in struk′ shən) *n.* **1** the act of teaching; education [The teacher spent his life in the *instruction* of others.] **2** something taught; lesson [I take swimming *instruction* at camp.] —*pl.* **in·struc′ tions**

in·ven·tion (in ven′ shən) *n.* something invented [The light bulb is Edison's *invention*.] —*pl.* **in·ven′ tions**

in·vite (in vīt′) *v.* to ask to be one's guest [Ten people were *invited* to the party.] —**in·vit′ ed, in·vit′ ing**

i·ron (ī′ ərn) *n.* **1** a strong metal that can be formed into various shapes after being heated. **2** a device made of metal that is heated and used for pressing clothes.

it'll (it′ ′l) it will.

J

jar (jär) *n.* a container made of glass, pottery, or stone. —*pl.* **jars**

jar·ful (jär′ fool) *n.* as much as a jar can hold [We opened a *jarful* of olives.] —*pl.* **jar′ fuls**

jer·sey (jur′ zē) *n.* a blouse, shirt, etc. made of a soft, knitted cloth. —*pl.* **jer′ seys**

jock·ey (jäk′ ē) *n.* a person who rides horses in races. —*pl.* **jock′ eys**

join (join) *v.* to become a member of [She *joined* our club.] —**joined, join′ ing**

joint (joint) *n.* a place where two bones are joined [His elbow *joint* was sore after the baseball game.] —*pl.* **joints**

jour·ney (jur′ nē) *n.* a trip. —*pl.* **jour′ neys**

judge (juj) *n.* an official who hears cases in a law court and makes decisions on them [The *judge* sentenced the guilty person.] —*pl.* **judg′ es** ♦*v.* to hear cases and make decisions in a law court [The prisoner was *judged* and sentenced.] —**judged, judg′ ing**

juic·y (joo′ sē) *adj.* full of liquid [I ate a *juicy* plum.] —**juic′ i·er, juic′ i·est**

jun·gle (jung′ g'l) *n.* land thickly covered with trees, as in the tropics. —*pl.* **jun′ gles**

K

kind·ness (kīnd′ nis) *n.* the condition of being helpful or generous [We thanked him for his *kindness*.]

L

la·dy (lā′ dē) *n.* a woman, —*pl.* **la′ dies**

lamp (lamp) *n.* a thing for giving light. —*pl.* **lamps**

lan·tern (lan′ tərn) *n.* a case of glass, paper, etc., holding a light and protecting it from wind and rain. —*pl.* **lan′ terns**

late·ly (lāt′ lē) *adv.* recently.

launch (lônch) *v.* to send off into space [We saw them *launch* the rocket.] —**launched, launch′ ing**

laun·dry (lôn′ drē) *n.* clothes that have been or are about to be washed.

law (lô) *n.* any rule people are expected to obey [Is there a *law* against jaywalking?] —*pl.* **laws**

lawn (lôn) *n.* ground covered with grass that is cut short. —*pl.* **lawns**

law·yer (lô′ yər) *n.* a person whose profession is giving advice on law. —*pl.* **law′ yers**

leash (lēsh) *n.* a strap or chain to hold a dog. —*pl.* **leash′ es**

least (lēst) *adj.* smallest in size, amount, or importance [I haven't the *least* interest in the matter.]

leave (lēv) *v.* to go away or go from. —**left, leav′ing**

lec·ture (lek′ chər) *n.* a talk on a subject to an audience or class. —*pl.* **lec′ tures**

left (left) *adj.; adv.* opposite of right [Raise your *left* hand.]

leg·is·la·ture (lej′ is lā′ chər) *n.* a group of people who make laws. —*pl.* **leg′ is·la′ tures**

li·brar·y (lī′ brer′ ē) *n.* a place where books are kept for reading or borrowing [I took out four books from the *library.*] —*pl.* **li′ brar′ ies**

lie (lī) *v.* **1** to stretch one's body in a flat position. **2** to be in a flat position [The book is *lying* on the table.] —**lay, lain, ly′ ing**

like·ly (līk′ lē) *adj.* to be expected [A storm is *likely* before noon.] —**like′ li·er, like′ li·est**

limp (limp) *v.* to walk in an uneven way because of a lame leg. —**limped, limp′ ing**

line (līn) *n.* **1** a cord, rope, string, etc. **2** a wire or pipe for carrying electricity, water, gas, etc. **3** a long thin mark [Put a *line* under the correct answer.] **4** a row of persons or things [There was a long *line* of people waiting to get in.] —*pl.* **lines**

live·ly (līv′ lē) *adj.* full of energy [We have six *lively* puppies.] —**live′ li·er, live′ li·est**

lodge (läj) *n.* a small house with a special purpose [We stayed at a hunting *lodge.*] —*pl.* **lodg′ es** ◆*v.* to live at a place for a time [My brother *lodged* with my uncle when he went to college.] —**lodged, lodg′ ing**

lone·li·ness (lōn′ lē nis) *n.* unhappiness at being alone [Her *loneliness* made her cry.]

lone·ly (lōn′ lē) *adj.* unhappy at being away from friends or family [Billy was *lonely* at camp.] —**lone′ li·er, lone′ li·est**

loose (lōōs) *adj.* not tight or firmly fastened [That cap is *loose.*] —**loos′ er, loos′ est** —**loose′ ly** *adv.*

lose (lōōz) *v.* **1** to fail to keep. **2** to fail to win [We *lost* the football game.] —**lost, los′ ing**

lo·tion (lō′ shən) *n.* a liquid that keeps skin soft or heals it. —*pl.* **lo′ tions**

love·li·ness (luv′ lē nis) *n.* beauty [I saw the *loveliness* of the flowers.]

love·ly (luv′ lē) *adj.* very pleasing in looks or character [The flowers were *lovely.*] —**love′ li·er, love′ li·est**

M

mag·ni·fy (mag′ nə fī) *v.* to make something seem larger than it is [The microscope *magnifies* objects fifty times.] —**mag′ ni·fied, mag′ ni·fy·ing**

a	fat	ir	here	ou	out	zh	leisure
ā	ape	ī	bite, fire	u	up	ng	ring
ä	car, lot	ō	go	ʉr	fur		a *in* ago
e	ten	ô	law, horn	ch	chin		e *in* agent
er	care	oi	oil	sh	she	ə =	i *in* unity
ē	even	oo	look	th	thin		o *in* collect
i	hit	o͞o	tool	th	then		u *in* focus

man (man) *n.* an adult, male human being. —*pl.* **men**

man·u·fac·ture (man′ yə fak′ chər) *v.* to make goods. —**man′ u·fac′ tured, man′ u·fac′ tur·ing**

map (map) *n.* a drawing or chart of all or part of the earth's surface. —*pl.* **maps** ♦*v.* to make a map of [Lewis and Clark *mapped* western America.] —**mapped, map′ ping**

mar·ble (mär′ b'l) *n.* **1** a kind of limestone. **2** a little ball of stone, glass, or clay. —*pl.* **mar′ bles** ♦*adj.* made of marble.

march (märch) *n.* a steady walk [The soldiers' *march* was very tiring.] —*pl.* **march′ es**

match (mach) *n.* a stick of wood or cardboard treated so it catches fire when rubbed. —*pl.* **match′ es**

mean (mēn) *v.* to have in mind as a purpose; intend [He *meant* to go, but changed his mind.] —**meant, mean′ ing**

meas·ure·ment (mezh′ ər mənt) *n.* size or amount found by using a measuring tool, such as a yardstick [The *measurement* is made in inches.] —*pl.* **meas′ ure·ments**

meat (mēt) *n.* the flesh of animals used as food. —*pl.* **meats**

mer·ry (mer′ ē) *adj.* filled with fun and laughter; cheerful [We had a *merry* party.] —**mer′ ri·er, mer′ ri·est** —**mer′ ri·ly** *adv.*

mes·sage (mes′ ij) *n.* a piece of information sent from one person to another [They got a *message* by telegram.] —*pl.* **mes′ sag·es**

min·i·a·ture (min′ ē ə chər) *adj.* that is a very small copy or model [I have a *miniature* railroad.]

mis·be·have (mis′ bi hāv′) *v.* to behave in a bad way [The spoiled baby *misbehaved.*] —**mis′ be·haved′, mis′ be·hav′ ing**

mis·con·duct (mis kän′ dukt) *n.* bad or wrong behavior [He was accused of *misconduct.*]

mis·in·form (mis in fôrm′) *v.* to give wrong facts to [I was *misinformed* about the bus schedule.] —**mis·in·formed′, mis·in·form′ ing**

mis·lay (mis lā′) *v.* to put something in a place and then forget where [I *mislaid* my glasses.] —**mis·laid′, mis·lay′ ing**

mis·lead (mis lēd′) *v.* to lead in a wrong direction [That old map will *mislead* you.] —**mis·led′, mis·lead′ ing**

mis·print (mis′ print) *n.* a mistake in printing [A *misprint* was on every page.] —*pl.* **mis·prints′**

mis·quote (mis kwōt′) *v.* to quote wrongly. —**mis·quot′ ed, mis·quot′ ing**

mis·read (mis rēd′) *v.* to read in the wrong way [Did you *misread* the directions?] —**mis·read** (mis red′), **mis·read′ ing**

mis·spell (mis spel′) *v.* to spell incorrectly [We all *misspelled* that word.] — **mis·spelled′, mis·spell′ ing**

mist (mist) *n.* a thin water vapor that can be seen in the air and that blurs the vision [There is a *mist* along the river bank in the morning.]

mis·treat (mis trēt′) *v.* to treat badly. —**mis·treat′ ed, mis·treat′ ing**

mis·un·der·stand (mis′ un dər stand′) *v.* to understand wrong; to give a wrong meaning to [They *misunderstood* the teacher's words.] —**mis′·un·der·stood′, mis′ un·der·stand′ ing**

mis·use (mis yōōz′) *v.* to use in a wrong way —**mis·used′, mis·us′ ing**

mix·ture (miks′ chər) *n.* something made by mixing [Punch is a *mixture* of fruit juices.] —*pl.* **mix′ tures**

mois·ture (mois′ chər) *n.* liquid causing a dampness.

mo·ment (mō′ mənt) *n.* a very short period of time [Let us pause for a *moment*.] —*pl.* **mo·ments**

mon·ey (mun′ ē) *n.* metal coins or paper bills to take the place of these issued by a government for use in buying and selling.

mop (mäp) *n.* a bundle of rags or yarn fastened to a stick used for washing floors. ✦*v.* to wash or wipe with a mop [Sailors often *mop* the deck.] —**mopped, mop′ ping**

mope (mōp) *v.* to be gloomy and dull [Rainy days make me *mope*.] —**moped, mop′ ing**

mo·tion (mō′ shən) *n.* movement [The car made a forward *motion*.] —*pl.* **mo′ tions**

moun·tain (moun′ t'n) *n.* a very high hill. —*pl.* **moun′ tains**

mul·ti·pli·ca·tion (mul′ tə pli kā′ shən) *n.* adding a figure to itself a certain number of times. —*pl.* **mul′ ti·pli·ca′ tions**

mul·ti·ply (mul′ tə plī) *v.* to repeat a figure a number of times [*Multiply* 10 by 4 to get 40.] —**mul′ ti·plied, mul′ ti·ply·ing**

must·n't (mus′ 'nt) must not.

N

na·tion (nā′ shən) *n.* a state or country. —*pl.* **na′ tions**

na·ture (nā′ chər) *n.* everything in the physical world that is not made by humans [Are you a *nature* lover?]

naugh·ty (nôt′ ē) *adj.* not behaving; disobedient [The *naughty* puppy made a mess.] —**naugh′ ti·er, naugh′ ti·est** —**naugh′ ti·ly** *adv.*

neat (nēt) *adj.* clean and in good order [His room was very *neat*.]

neigh·bor (nā′ bər) *n.* a person who lives by someone else [The closest *neighbor* lives three miles away.] —*pl.* **neigh′ bors**

nice (nīs) *adj.* good, pleasant, agreeable, pretty, kind, polite, etc. [That is a *nice* sweater.] —**nic′ er, nic′ est** —**nice′ ly** *adv.*

niece (nēs) *n.* the daughter of one's brother or sister. —*pl.* **niec′ es**

noise (noiz) *n.* sound, especially a loud sound [The *noise* of the fireworks woke up the baby.] —*pl.* **nois′ es**

nurse (nʉrs) *n.* a person trained to care for sick people and help doctors. —*pl.* **nurs′ es**

O

oc·cu·py (äk′ yə pī) *v.* to live in [They have *occupied* that house for fifteen years.] —**oc′ cu·pied, oc′ cu·py·ing**

o'clock (ə kläk′) *adv.* of the clock [It is twelve *o'clock* midnight.]

a	fat	ir	here	ou	out	zh	leisure
ā	ape	ī	bite, fire	u	up	ng	ring
ä	car, lot	ō	go	ʉr	fur		a *in* ago
e	ten	ô	law, horn	ch	chin		e *in* agent
er	care	oi	oil	sh	she	ə = i *in* unity
ē	even	oo	look	th	thin		o *in* collect
i	hit	ōō	tool	th	then		u *in* focus

of·fice (ôf′ is) *n.* the place where a certain kind of business is carried on [This is a lawyer's *office*.] —*pl.* **of′ fic·es**

of·fi·cer (ôf′ ə sər) *n.* **1** a person holding some office. **2** a member of the police force. —*pl.* **of′ fi·cers**

oil (oil) *n.* a greasy liquid that burns.

o·pin·ion (ə pin′ yən) *n.* a belief that is not based on what is certain, but on what one thinks to be likely [In my *opinion*, it will rain tomorrow.] —*pl.* **o·pin′ ions**

or·ange (ôr′ inj *or* är′ inj) *n.* **1** a round citrus fruit with a reddish-yellow skin. **2** a reddish yellow color. —*pl.* **or′ ang·es**

os·trich (ôs′ trich) *n.* a large bird of Africa and southwestern Asia with a long neck and legs. —*pl.* **os′ trich·es**

ought (ôt) *a helping verb used with infinitives and meaning:* **1** to be forced by what is right or necessary [You *ought* to apologize.] **2** likely or expected [It *ought* to be over soon.]

ounce (ouns) *n.* a unit of weight. —*pl.* **ounc′ es**

out·law (out′ lô) *n.* a criminal [The *outlaw* ran from the police.] —*pl.* **out′ laws**

P

pack·age (pak′ ij) *n.* a wrapped parcel [We got a large *package* in the mail.] —*pl.* **pack′ ag·es**

page (pāj) *n.* an entire leaf in a book, newspaper, etc. [This *page* is torn.] —*pl.* **pag′ es**

pas·ture (pas′ chər) *n.* land where grass and plants grow and where cattle, sheep, etc. can feed. —*pl.* **pas′ tures**

patch (pach) *n.* a piece of cloth, metal, etc. used to mend a hole or worn spot. ◆*v.* to put a patch on [I *patched* my old sweater.] —**patched, patch′ ing**

pause (pôz) *n.* a short stop in speech or work [He made a dramatic *pause* in his speech.] —*pl.* **paus′ es** ◆*v.* to stop for a short time [The crying baby *paused* for breath.] —**paused, paus′ ing**

pave·ment (pāv′ mənt) *n.* a paved road or sidewalk. —*pl.* **pave′ ments**

paw (pô) *n.* the foot of an animal that has claws [Our dog hurt his front *paw*.] —*pl.* **paws**

peace·ful (pēs′ fəl) *adj.* quiet; calm [They played a *peaceful* game of checkers.] —**peace′ ful·ly** *adv.*

peach (pēch) *n.* a round, juicy fruit with fuzzy skin. —*pl.* **peach′ es**

peak (pēk) *n.* the pointed top of a mountain [He climbed to the *peak* of the mountain.] —*pl.* **peaks**

pen·cil (pen′ s'l) *n.* a long, thin piece of wood, metal, etc. with a center stick of graphite or crayon for writing or drawing. —*pl.* **pen′ cils**

peo·ple (pē′ p'l) *n.* human beings.

pe·ri·od (pir′ ē əd) *n.* **1** a portion of time into which a game, a school day, etc. is divided. **2** the mark of punctuation used at the end of most sentences and after abbreviations. —*pl.* **pe′ ri·ods**

pick·le (pik′ ′l) *n.* a vegetable preserved in salt water, vinegar, or spicy liquid. —*pl.* **pick′ les**

pic·ture (pik′ chər) *n.* a likeness of a person, thing, or scene made by drawing, painting, or photography. —*pl.* **pic′ tures**

piece (pēs) *n.* one of a set of things [She lost a chess *piece*.] —*pl.* **piec′ es**

pi·lot (pī′ lət) *n.* a person who flies an aircraft [He wants to be a helicopter *pilot*.] —*pl.* **pi′ lots**

pine (pīn) *n.* **1** an evergreen tree with cones and leaves shaped like needles. **2** the wood of this tree. —*pl.* **pines**

pitch (pich) *v.* to throw or toss [*Pitch* the garbage in the can.] —**pitched, pitch′ ing**

pit·y (pit′ ē) *n.* a feeling of sorrow for another's trouble [She felt *pity* for the caged lion.] —*pl.* **pit′ ies** ♦*v.* to feel sorrow for [They *pitied* the lost animal.] —**pit′ ied, pit′ y·ing**

plan (plan) *n.* a thought-out method of doing something [We made our vacation *plans* early.] —*pl.* **plans**

plane (plān) *n.* a man-made craft that flies through the air. —*pl.* **planes**

plant (plant) *n.* any living thing that cannot move and makes its own food by photosynthesis. —*pl.* **plants**

plate·ful (plāt′ fool) *n.* as much as a plate will hold [I ate a *plateful* of spaghetti.] —*pl.* **plate′ fuls**

pledge (plej) *n.* a promise or agreement [They said the *pledge* of allegiance to the flag.] —*pl.* **pledg′ es**

plen·ty (plen′ tē) *n.* a supply that is large enough; all that is needed [We have *plenty* of help.]

plot (plät) *v.* to plan secretly [They *plotted* to rob the bank.] —**plot′ ted, plot′ ting**

point (point) *n.* a sharp end [The needle has a sharp *point*.] —*pl.* **points** ♦*v.* to aim [The compass needle *pointed* north.] —**point′ ed, point′ ing**

poi·son (poi′ z'n) *n.* a substance that causes illness or death. —*pl.* **poi′ sons** ♦*adj.* is or contains a poison [*poison* gas].

po·lite·ness (pə līt′ nəs) *n.* the state of being polite.

porch (pôrch) *n.* an open room outside a building [We sat on the screened *porch* after lunch.] —*pl.* **porch′ es**

pos·ture (päs′ chər) *n.* the way one holds the body [Good *posture* is important.]

pound (pound) *n.* a unit of weight equal to 16 ounces [I bought a *pound* of candy.] —*pl.* **pounds**

pow·er (pou′ ər) *n.* strength or force [The *power* of the storm was frightening.] —*pl.* **pow′ ers**

pre·pare (pri par′) *v.* to get ready [He *prepared* for the test by studying hard.] —**pre·pared′, pre·par′ ing**

pres·ent (prez′ 'nt) *adj.* **1** being at a certain place; not absent [Is everyone *present* today?] **2** of this time, not past or future. *n.* **1** this time; now. **2** something given; gift [He gave me a *present*.] —*pl.* **pres·ents**

pres·i·dent (prez′ i dənt) *n.* the highest officer of a company, club, government, etc. —*pl.* **pres′ i·dents**

price·less (prīs′ lis) *adj.* too valuable to be measured by price [The painting is *priceless*.]

a	fat	ir	here	ou	out	zh	leisure
ā	ape	ī	bite, fire	u	up	ng	ring
ä	car, lot	ō	go	ʉr	fur		a *in* ago
e	ten	ô	law, horn	ch	chin		e *in* agent
er	care	oi	oil	sh	she	ə =	i *in* unity
ē	even	oo	look	th	thin		o *in* collect
i	hit	o͞o	tool	*th*	then		u *in* focus

prin·ci·pal (prin′ sə pəl) *n.* the head of a school. —*pl.* **prin′ ci·pals**

prod·uct (präd′ əkt) *n.* something produced by nature or by human beings [Wood is a natural *product.*]

prom·ise (präm′ is) *n.* an agreement to do or not to do something. —*pl.* **prom′ is·es** ♦*v.* to make a promise [I *promised* to visit her soon.] —**prom′ ised, prom′ is·ing**

proud (proud) *adj.* feeling or causing pride or pleasure [I was *proud* of my drawing.] —**proud′ er, proud′ est,** —**proud′ ly** *adv.*

prove (proov) *v.* to show that something is true or correct [The experiment *proved* she was right.] —**proved, prov′ ing**

prowl (proul) *v.* to roam in a secret way [Our cat *prowls* for mice.] —**prowled, prowl′ ing**

punc·tu·a·tion (pungk′ choo wā′ shən) *n.* the use of commas, periods, etc. in writing [We study *punctuation* in school.]

punc·ture (pungk′ chər) *v.* to pierce [*Puncture* the balloon.] —**punc′ tured, punc′ tur·ing**

pur·ple (pʉr′ p'l) *n.* a color that is a mixture of red and blue.

Q

ques·tion (kwes′ chən) *n.* **1** something asked [The curious girl asked a *question.*] **2** a matter to be considered; problem [It's not a *question* of money.] —*pl.* **ques′ tions** ♦*v.* to ask questions of [The police officer *questioned* him.] —**ques′ tioned, ques′ tion·ing**

R

rail·way (rāl′ wā) *n.* tracks for the wheels of a train. —*pl.* **rail′ ways**

rare (rer) *adj.* not often found; not common [The zoo has many *rare* birds.] —**rar′ er, rar′ est** —**rare′ ly** *adv.*

raw·hide (rô′ hīd) *n.* a cattle hide that has been made into leather.

re·ceive (ri sēv′) *v.* to take or get what has been given or sent [He *received* many presents.] —**re·ceived′, re·ceiv′ ing**

re·fuse (ri fyooz′) *v.* to say one will not take or do something [He *refused* to take his medicine.] —**re·fused′, re·fus′ ing**

rein·deer (rān′ dir) *n.* a large deer found in northern regions. —*pl.* **rein′ deer**

re·joice (ri jois′) *v.* to be or make happy [We *rejoiced* at the news.] —**re·joiced′, re·joic′ ing**

re·lief (ri lēf′) *n.* **1** a lessening of pain, discomfort, or worry [This medicine gives *relief* from coughing.] **2** help given to poor people, flood victims, etc. [The Red Cross gave *relief* after the hurricane.]

rel·ish (rel′ ish) *n.* pickles, olives, etc. —*pl.* **rel′ ish·es**

re·mem·ber (ri mem′ bər) *v.* to think of again. —**re·mem′ bered, re·mem′ ber·ing**

rent (rent) *n.* money paid at regular times for the use of a house, office, land, etc. ♦*v.* to get or give the use of a house, land, etc. in return for regular payment of money. —**rent′ ed, rent′ ing**

re·ply (ri plī′) *v.* to answer by saying something [She *replied* to the question.] —**re·plied′, re·ply′ ing**

re·port·er (ri pôrt′ ər) *n.* a person who reports news. —*pl.* **re·port′ ers**

re·trieve (ri trēv′) *v.* to find and bring back [Our dog *retrieves* balls.] —**re·trieved′, re·triev′ ing**

rip (rip) *v.* to tear apart [I *ripped* the hem of my skirt.] —**ripped, rip′ ping**

rob (räb) *v.* to steal by using force or threats [The criminals *robbed* the bank.] —**robbed, rob′ bing**

robe (rōb) *n.* a long outer garment, as a bathrobe. —*pl.* **robes** ◆*v.* to dress in a long garment [The king was *robed* in red velvet.] —**robed, rob′ ing**

rot (rät) *v.* to fall apart or spoil [A dead tree will *rot*.] —**rot′ ted, rot′ ting**

rough (ruf) *adj.* not smooth or level; uneven [The wagon ride was *rough*.] —**rough′ er, rough′ est** —**rough′ ly** *adv.*

rust·y (rus′ tē) *adj.* coated with rust. —**rust′ i·er, rust′ i·est**

S

sad (sad) *adj.* feeling unhappy [We were *sad* to see her go.] —**sad′ der, sad′ dest** —**sad′ ly** *adv.* —**sad·ness** *n.*

sad·ness (sad′ nis) *n.* the feeling of unhappiness; sorrow [The loss of his pet caused him great *sadness*.]

safe (sāf) *adj.* free from harm or danger [I feel *safe* at home.] —**saf′ er, saf′ est** —**safe′ ly** *adv.*

sail·or (sāl′ ər) *n.* an enlisted person in the navy. —*pl.* **sail′ ors**

sale (sāl) *n.* **1** the act of selling [The clerk made ten *sales* today.] **2** a special selling of goods at prices lower than usual [The store held a clearance *sale*.] —*pl.* **sales**

sam·ple (sam′ p'l) *n.* specimen or example [He showed me a *sample* of his typing.]

—*pl.* **sam′ ples** ◆*v.* to test by trying a sample [He *sampled* the grapes.] —**sam′ pled, sam′ pling**

sand·box (sand′ bäks) *n.* a box filled with sand. —*pl.* **sand′ box·es**

sand·wich (sand′ wich *or* san′ wich) *n.* slices of bread with meat, cheese, etc. between them. —*pl.* **sand′ wich·es**

sat·is·fy (sat′ is fī) *v.* to meet the needs of; to please [This meal will *satisfy* him.] —**sat′ is·fied, sat′ is·fy·ing**

sauce (sôs) *n.* a liquid or dressing used to make food tastier [Put lots of *sauce* on my spaghetti.] —*pl.* **sauc′ es**

sau·cer (sô′ sər) *n.* a small dish for a cup to rest on [She spilled coffee in the *saucer*.] —*pl.* **sau′ cers**

sau·sage (sô′ sij) *n.* meat, chopped up, seasoned, and stuffed into a tube [I like *sausage* on my pizza.] —*pl.* **sau′ sag·es**

saw·dust (sô′ dust) *n.* tiny bits of wood formed in sawing wood.

scar (skär) *n.* a mark left on the skin when a cut or burn has healed. ◆*v.* to mark with or form a scar [The cut *scarred* his knee.] —**scarred, scar′ ring**

a	fat	ir	here	ou	out	zh	leisure
ā	ape	ī	bite, fire	u	up	ng	ring
ä	car, lot	ō	go	ʉr	fur		a *in* ago
e	ten	ô	law, horn	ch	chin		e *in* agent
er	care	oi	oil	sh	she	ə =	i *in* unity
ē	even	oo	look	th	thin		o *in* collect
i	hit	ōō	tool	th	then		u *in* focus

scare (sker) *v.* to make or become afraid; frighten [The mask *scared* him.] —**scared, scar' ing**

scent (sent) *n.* a faint smell; odor [I like the *scent* of freshly cut hay.] —*pl.* **scents**

sci·en·tist (sī' ən tist) *n.* an expert in science. —*pl.* **sci' en·tists**

score (skôr) *n.* the number of points made in a game [Her highest bowling *score* was 110.] —*pl.* **scores** ◆*v.* to make points in a game [The hockey player *scored* two goals.] —**scored, scor' ing**

score·less (skôr' lis) *adj.* not having scored any points.

scrap (skrap) *n.* a small piece; bit [I dropped a *scrap* of paper.] —*pl.* **scraps**

scrape (skrāp) *v.* to scratch or rub something from. ◆*n.* a scraped place [I have a painful *scrape* on my ankle.] —*pl.* **scrapes**

scratch (skrach) *v.* to rub with fingernails to relieve itching [He *scratched* a mosquito bite.] —**scratched, scratch' ing**

scrawl (skrôl) *v.* to write hastily [She *scrawled* a note to her friend.] —**scrawled, scrawl' ing**

scraw·ny (skrô' nē) *adj.* skinny. —**scraw' ni·er, scraw' ni·est**

scream (skrēm) *v.* to give a loud, shrill cry, as in fright or pain. —**screamed, scream' ing** ◆*n.* a loud, shrill cry or sound. —*pl.* **screams**

scrub (skrub) *v.* to clean by rubbing hard [*Scrub* the floors.] —**scrubbed, scrub' bing**

sec·re·tar·y (sek' rə ter' ē) *n.* a person whose work is keeping records, etc. for a person or organization. —*pl.* **sec' re·tar' ies**

sec·tion (sek' shən) *n.* a part cut off [Eat a *section* of an orange.] —*pl.* **sec' tions**

se·cure (si kyōōr') *adj.* free from fear, care, or worry; safe [I feel *secure* about my grades.] —**se·cure' ly** *adv.*

seek (sēk) *v.* to try to find [Miners went west to *seek* gold.] —**sought, seek' ing**

sense·less (sens' lis) *adj.* stupid, foolish, meaningless [His mumbling was *senseless*.] —**sense' less·ly** *adv.*

sen·tence (sen' t'ns) *n.* a group of words used to tell or ask something ["I saw John'' is a *sentence*.] —*pl.* **sen' tenc·es**

sep·a·rate (sep' ər it) *adj.* set apart from the others; not joined [The garage is *separate* from the house.] —**sep' a·rate·ly** *adv.*

serve (surv) *v.* to offer food or drink to [The waiter *served* our dinner.] —**served, serv' ing**

shame·ful (shām' fəl) *adj.* bringing shame or disgrace [Stealing is *shameful*.] —**shame' ful·ly** *adv.*

shape·less (shāp' lis) *adj.* without a well-formed shape [The old rag doll was *shapeless*.]

share (sher) *v.* to divide and give out [He *shared* his candy with his friends.] —**shared, shar' ing** *n.* a part that each one gets [They want their *share* of the pie.] —*pl.* **shares**

shawl (shôl) *n.* a large piece of cloth worn over the shoulders. —*pl.* **shawls**

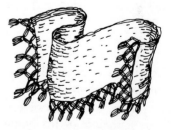

she's (shēz) **1** she is. **2** she has.

shield (shēld) *v.* to protect [Trees *shield* us from storms.] —**shield' ed, shield' ing**

◆*n.* armour used to ward off blows [The knight used his *shield* in battle.] —*pl.* **shields**

shine (shīn) *v.* **1** to be bright or give off light [The sun was *shining.*] **2** to make something give off light [*Shine* your flashlight under the bed.] —**shone** *or* **shined, shin′ ing**

ship (ship) *n.* any vessel, larger than a boat, for traveling on water. —*pl.* **ships** ◆*v.* to send in a ship, train, or plane [The cargo was *shipped* from New York.] —**shipped, ship′ ping**

ship·ment (ship′ mənt) *n.* goods that are shipped or transported. —*pl.* **ship′ ments**

shoot (shoot) *v.* **1** to send out with force from a gun, bow, etc. **2** to throw or send out swiftly and with force. —**shot, shoot′ ing**

should (shood) *v.* a helping verb used with other verbs when speaking of something that is likely to happen or of something that one ought to do [The show *should* begin soon. We *should* go now.]

shoul·der (shōl′ dər) *n.* the part of the body to which an arm or foreleg is connected. —*pl.* **shoul′ ders**

should·n't (shood′ ′nt) should not.

shout (shout) *v.* to speak in a loud voice [She *shouted* across the yard.] —**shout′ ed, shout′ ing**

sig·na·ture (sig′ nə chər) *n.* a person's name as he or she has written it. —*pl.* **sig′ na·tures**

sil·ly (sil′ ē) *adj.* not showing good sense [The *silly* dog barked at its reflection.] —**sil′ li·er, sil′ li·est**

sim·ple (sim′ p'l) *adj.* easy [That is a *simple* task.] —**sim′ pler, sim′ plest**

sin·cere (sin sir′) *adj.* honest; truthful; not pretending [Are you *sincere* in wanting to help?] —**sin·cer′ er, sin·cer′ est** —**sin·cere′ ly** *adv.*

sin·gle (sing′ g'l) *adj.* one only [The carriage was drawn by a *single* horse.]

sketch (skech) *v.* to make a simple drawing of [He *sketched* a picture of the house.] —**sketched, sketch′ ing**

skin (skin) *n.* **1** the tissue covering the body of persons and animals. **2** the outer covering of some fruits and vegetables. ◆*v.* to remove the skin from [I *skinned* my elbow by falling.] —**skinned, skin′ ning**

sleeve·less (slēv′ lis) *adj.* without sleeves.

sleigh (slā) *n.* a carriage with runners that moves on snow or ice. —*pl.* **sieighs**

slide (slīd) *v.* to move easily along a surface [Children *slide* on the ice.] —**slid** (slid), **slid′ ing**

slim (slim) *adj.* thin. —**slim′ mer, slim′ mest** —**slim′ ness** *n.*

smart (smart) *adj.* intelligent or clever. —**smar′ ter, smar′ test**

smudge (smuj) *n.* a dirty spot; smear. —*pl.* **smudg′ es**

snap (snap) *v.* to make a sharp, cracking sound [She *snapped* her fingers.] —**snapped, snap′ ping** ◆*n.* a fastening that closes with a clicking sound [Some jeans have a *snap* at the waist.] —*pl.* **snaps**

a	fat	ir	here	ou	out	zh	leisure
ā	ape	ī	bite, fire	u	up	ng	ring
ä	car, lot	ō	go	ur	fur		a *in* ago
e	ten	ô	law, horn	ch	chin		e *in* agent
er	care	oi	oil	sh	she	ə = i *in* unity
ē	even	oo	look	th	thin		o *in* collect
i	hit	ōō	tool	th	then		u *in* focus

sneeze (snēz) *v.* to blow breath in a sudden, uncontrolled way [She *sneezed* in the dusty room.] —**sneezed, sneez′ ing** ♦*n.* an act of sneezing [Her *sneeze* was very loud.] —*pl.* **sneez′ es**

snore (snôr) *v.* to breathe noisily while sleeping [He *snored* so loudly it woke us up.] —**snored, snor′ ing**

soc·cer (säk′ ər) *n.* a football game in which a round ball is moved by kicking.

soft (sôft) *adj.* **1** not hard or firm [This pillow is *soft*.] **2** smooth [*soft* skin]. —**soft′ ly** *adv.* —**soft′ ness** *n.*

soil (soil) *n.* the top layer of earth [Cover the seeds with *soil*.] —*pl.* **soils** ♦*v.* to make or become dirty —**soiled, soil′ ing**

sore (sôr) *adj.* giving pain, aching [I have a *sore* toe.] —**sor′ er, sor′ est** —**sore′ ness** *n.*

sought (sôt) *past tense and past participle of* **seek**

sour (sour) *adj.* having the sharp taste of lemon juice or vinegar [Unripe fruit tastes *sour*.] —**sour′ ly** *adv.*

space (spās) *n.* **1** the area that contains all things in the universe [All the stars exist in *space*.] **2** the area inside of something or between things [That closet has enough *space*.] —*pl.* **spa′ ces**

speak (spēk) *v.* to say something [Please *speak* more quietly.] —**spoke, spo′ ken, speak′ ing**

spice (spīs) *n.* any vegetable substance that gives flavor or smell to food [Pepper is a useful *spice*.] —*pl.* **spices**

spi·der (spī dər) *n.* a small animal with eight legs that makes webs. —*pl.* **spi′ ders**

spin·ach (spin′ ich) *n.* a vegetable with large, dark-green leaves.

spoil (spoil) *v.* to make worthless or rotten [Ink stains *spoiled* the paper.] —**spoiled, spoil′ ing**

sponge (spunj) *n.* anything full of holes that can soak up liquid [He cleaned the counter with a *sponge*.] —*pl.* **spong′ es**

spook·y (spook′ ē) *adj.* of, like, or suggesting a ghost. —**spook′ i·er, spook′ i·est**

sprawl (sprôl) *v.* to sit or lie with arms and legs spread out. —**sprawled, sprawl′ ing**

sprin·kle (spring′ k′l) *v.* to scatter in drops or bits [*Sprinkle* salt on the egg.] —**sprin′ kled, sprin′ kling**

sprout (sprout) *v.* to begin to grow [Buds *sprouted* on the roses.] —**sprout′ ed, sprout′ ing**

squir·rel (skwʉr′ əl) *n.* a small, bushytailed animal that lives in trees. —*pl.* **squir′ rels**

stage (stāj) *n.* a platform or area on which plays, speeches, etc. are given. —*pl.* **stag′ es**

stair (ster) *n.* one of a series of steps going up or down. —*pl.* **stairs** a flight of steps.

stamp (stamp) *n.* a small piece of paper printed and sold by a government for sticking on a letter, etc. as proof that proper postage has been paid. —*pl.* **stamps**

star (stär) *n.* a heavenly body seen as a small light at night. —*pl.* **stars** ♦*v.* to play an important part [The actress *starred* in four movies.] —**starred, star′ ring**

stare (ster) *v.* to look steadily at [They *stared* at his Halloween costume.] —**stared, star′ ing**

sta·tion (stā′ shən) *n.* **1** a regular stopping place for a bus or train [I'll pick you up at the bus *station*.] **2** a place that sends out radio or televison programs [WXYZ is a good radio *station*.] —*pl.* **sta′ tions**

stead·y (sted′ ē) *adj.* not shaky [Hold the ladder *steady*.] —**stead′ i·er, stead′ i·est** ♦*v.* to make or become steady [*Steady* that boat, please.] —**stead′ ied, stead′ y·ing,** —**stead′ i·ly** *adv.*

steak (stāk) *n.* a slice of meat, especially beef [They ate sirloin *steak* for dinner.] —*pl.* **steaks**

steep (stēp) *adj.* slanting sharply up or down [That hill is very *steep*.] —**steep′er, steep′est**

step (step) *v.* to move by placing the foot forward, backward, sideways, up, or down [He *stepped* over the puddle.] —**stepped, step′ ping**

stitch (stich) *v.* to see [The doctor *stitched* his cut knee.] —**stitched, stitch′ ing**

sto·ry (stôr′ ē) *n.* a written or spoken tale. —*pl.* **sto′ ries**

stove (stōv) *n.* a device for cooking or heating by the use of gas, electricity, etc. —*pl.* **stoves**

strange (strānj) *adj.* peculiar, odd [He was wearing a *strange* costume.] —**strang′ er, strang′ est** —**strange′ ly** *adv.*

strap (strap) *n.* a narrow strip for holding things. —*pl.* **straps**

straw (strô) *n.* a tube used for sucking a drink [I sipped a soda through a *straw*.] —*pl.* **straws**

straw·ber·ry (strô′ ber′ ē) *n.* a small, red, juicy fruit. —*pl.* **straw′ ber′ ries**

stream (strēm) *n.* a flow of water such as a small river. —*pl.* **streams** ♦*v.* to flow in a stream. —**streamed, stream′ ing**

stretch (strech) *v.* to pull out to, or past, its full length [He *stretched* the rubber band until it broke.] —**stretched, stretch′ ing**

stu·dent (stood′ ′nt) *n.* a person who studies. —*pl.* **stu′ dents**

stud·y (stud′ ē) *v.* to read or think about so as to understand [We *studied* our lessons.] —**stud′ ied, stud′ y·ing**

sub·merge (səb murj′) *v.* to put, go, or stay under water [Whales can *submerge* for half an hour.] —**sub·merged′, sub·merg′ ing**

sub·trac·tion (səb trak′ shən) *n.* the act of subtracting one from another.

sub·way (sub′ wā) *n.* an underground electric railway. —*pl.* **sub′ ways**

sug·ges·tion (səg jes′ chən) *n.* something mentioned to think over [They made a *suggestion* to improve the park.] —*pl.* **sug·ges′ tions**

sup·ply (sə plī′) *v.* to give what is needed [The camp *supplies* sheets.] —**sup·plied′, sup·ply′ ing** ♦*n.* **1** the amount at hand [I have a large *supply* of paper.] **2 supplies,** *pl.* materials [school *supplies*]. —*pl.* **sup·plies′**

sure·ly (shoor′ lē) *adv.* without doubt; certainly [He will *surely* remember his promise.]

sur·prise (sər prīz′) *v.* to cause one to feel wonder by being unexpected [Her sudden anger *surprised* us.] —**sur·prised′, sur·pris′ ing.** ♦*n.* something that is not expected [The party will be a *surprise*.] —*pl.* **sur·pris′ es**

a	fat	ir	here	ou	out	zh	leisure
ā	ape	ī	bite, fire	u	up	ng	ring
ä	car, lot	ō	go	ur	fur		a *in* ago
e	ten	ô	law, horn	ch	chin		e *in* agent
er	care	oi	oil	sh	she	ə =	i *in* unity
ē	even	oo	look	th	thin		o *in* collect
i	hit	oo	tool	th	then		u *in* focus

sur·round (sə round′) *v.* to enclose [The police *surrounded* the criminals.] —**sur·round′ ed, sur·round′ ing**

switch (switch) *v.* to shift; change [Let's *switch* the party to tonight.] —**switched, switch′ ing**

T

ta·ble (tā′ b'l) *n.* **1** a piece of furniture with a flat top set on legs [Put the dishes on the kitchen *table*.] **2** a chart of facts and figures [Study the *table* in this book.] —*pl.* **ta′ bles**

tap (tap) *v.* to hit lightly [She *tapped* my shoulder.] —**tapped, tap′ ping**

tape (tāp) *n.* a strong strip used for binding or tying. ♦*v.* to tie with tape [The doctor *taped* my bad knee.] —**taped, tap′ ing**

taste·less (tāst′ lis) *adj.* without taste or flavor [Spaghetti is *tasteless* without sauce.]

teach (tēch) *v.* to help to learn how to do something [He *taught* us to skate.] —**taught, teach′ ing**

teach·er (tēch′ ər) *n.* a person who teaches. —*pl.* **teach′ ers**

team (tēm) *n.* a group of people working or playing together. —*pl.* **teams**

tem·per·a·ture (tem′ prə chər) *n.* the degree of hotness or coldness. —*pl.* **tem′ per·a·tures**

ten·der·ness (ten′ dər nəs) *n.* the state of being soft or loving.

thaw (thô) *v.* to melt [The snow *thawed*.] —**thawed, thaw′ ing**

there's (*th*erz) there is.

they'd (*th*ād) they would.

they'll (*th*āl) they will.

they're (*th*er) they are.

they've (*th*āv) they have.

thin (thin) *adj.* **1** lean, slender. **2** not deep and strong; weak [She spoke in a *thin* voice.] —**thin′ ner, thin′ nest** —**thin′ ly** *adv.*

think (thingk) *v.* to believe, expect, or imagine [They *think* they can come.] —**thought, think′ ing**

thor·ough (thur′ ō) *adj.* complete [Make a *thorough* search.]

though (*th*ō) *conj.* in spite of the fact that [*Though* it rained, we went.]

thou·sand (thou′ z'nd) *n., adj.* ten times one hundred [This tree is a *thousand* years old.] —*pl.* **thou′ sands**

thread (thred) *n.* a thin cord used in sewing. —*pl.* **threads**

through (thro͞o) *prep.* from side to side or end to end of [The nail went *through* the board.]

tick·le (tik′ 'l) *v.* to touch lightly, so as to cause twitching or laughter. —**tick′ led, tick′ ling**

ti·ger (ti′ gər) *n.* a large, fierce animal of the cat family, living in Asia. —*pl.* **ti′ gers**

ti·ny (tī′ nē) *adj.* very small [There is a *tiny* spot on the wall.] —**ti′ ni·er, ti′ ni·est**

tire·less (tīr′ lis) *adj.* does not become tired [She is a *tireless* worker.] —**tire′ less·ly** *adv.*

ton (tun) *n.* a U.S. measure of weight equal to 2,000 pounds. —*pl.* **tons**

touch (tuch) *v.* to use the hand or finger to feel something [He *touched* the wet paint.] —**touched, touch′ ing**

tough (tuf) *adj.* very difficult or hard [Shoveling snow is *tough* work.]

toward (tôrd) *prep.* in the direction of [The house faces *toward* the park.]

tow·er (tou′ ər) *n.* a building that is much higher than it is wide [The water *tower* was struck by lightning.] —*pl.* **tow′ ers**

trade (trād) *v.* to exchange [I'll *trade* my comic books for your football.] —**trad′ ed, trad′ ing**

train (trān) *n.* a line of railroad cars pulled by a locomotive. —*pl.* **trains**

treas·ure (trezh′ ər) *n.* money or jewels collected [Pirates used to bury stolen *treasure*.] —*pl.* **treas′ ures**

treas·ur·er (trezh′ ər ər) *n.* a person in charge of a treasury. —*pl.* **treas′ ur·ers**

treat (trēt) *v.* to deal with or act toward in a certain way [*Treat* the visitors with respect.] —**treat′ ed, treat′ ing** ◆ *n.* anything that gives pleasure [It was a *treat* to hear them sing.] —*pl.* **treats**

trim (trim) *v.* to make neat or tidy, especially by clipping [He *trimmed* his fingernails.] —**trimmed, trim′ ming**

trip (trip) *v.* to stumble or make stumble [She *tripped* over the rug.] —**tripped, trip′ ping**

tro·phy (trō′ fē) *n.* anything kept as a token of victory [The winning runner was given a silver *trophy*.] —*pl.* **tro′ phies**

trou·ble (trub′ ′l) *n.* a difficult or unhappy situation [We've never had *trouble* with our neighbors.] —*pl.* **trou′ bles**

trough (trôf) *n.* a long, narrow, open container from which animals eat or drink. —*pl.* **troughs**

tru·ly (trōo′ lē) *adv.* in fact; really [Are you *truly* sorry?]

truth (trōoth) *n.* that which is true; the real facts [Did the newspaper print the *truth* about you?] —*pl.* **truths**

try (trī) *v.* to make an effort [We must *try* to help them.] —**tried, try′ ing**

tub (tub) *n.* bathtub. —*pl.* **tubs**

tube (tōob) *n.* **1** a long, slender, hollow piece of material [We breathe through the bronchial *tubes*.] **2** a long, slender container with a screw cap at one end. —*pl.* **tubes**

tube·ful (tōob′ fool) *n.* a full tube of. —*pl.* **tube′ fuls**

tub·ful (tub′ fool) *n.* a full tub of. —*pl.* **tub′ fuls**

tur·tle (tur′ t'l) *n.* an animal with a soft body covered by a hard shell. —*pl.* **tur′ tles**

twin·kle (twing′ k'l) *v.* to shine with quick flashes of light; sparkle [Stars seem to *twinkle* in the sky.] —**twin′ kled, twin′ kling**

U

ug·ly (ug′ lē) *adj.* unpleasing to look at [That painting is *ugly*.] —**ug′ li·er, ug′ li·est**

a	fat	ir	here	ou	out	zh	leisure
ā	ape	ī	bite, fire	u	up	ng	ring
ä	car, lot	ō	go	ur	fur		a *in* ago
e	ten	ô	law, horn	ch	chin		e *in* agent
er	care	oi	oil	sh	she	ə =	i *in* unity
ē	even	oo	look	th	thin		o *in* collect
i	hit	ōo	tool	th	then		u *in* focus

un·a·ware (un ə wer′) *adj.* not aware [We were *unaware* of the danger.]

un·ex·pect·ed (un′ ik spek′ tid) *adj.* not expected; surprising, sudden [The gift was *unexpected*.] —**un·ex·pec′ ted·ly** *adv.*

un·fas·ten (un fas′ 'n) *v.* to open. —**un·fas′ tened, un·fas′ ten·ing**

un·fin′ ished (un fin′ isht) *adj.* not finished or completed [The statue is still *unfinished*.]

un·fold (un fōld′) *v.* to open and spread out something that has been folded [*Unfold* the map carefully.] —**un·fold′ ed, un·fold′ ing**

un·friend·ly (un frend′ lē) *adj.* not friendly; showing bad feelings [That man seems very *unfriendly*.]

un·hurt (un hurt′) *adj.* not injured [He was *unhurt* in the fall.]

un·im·por·tant (un′ im por′ t'nt) *adj.* not important, minor [The message was *unimportant*.]

un·in·ter·est·ing (un in′ tər ist ing) *adj.* not interesting; dull [This book is very *uninteresting*.]

un·known (un nōn′) *adj.* not known, seen, or heard before [The writer of that poem is *unknown*.]

un·law·ful (un lô′ fəl) *adj.* against the law, illegal [Polluting the water is *unlawful*.] —**un·law′ ful·ly** *adv.*

un·nec·es·sar·y (un nes′ ə ser′ ē) *adj.* not necessary; needless. [His trip to the store was *unnecessary*.] —**un·nec′ es·sar′ i·ly** *adv.*

un·pop·u·lar (un päp′ yə lər) *adj.* not popular; not liked by most people [He was *unpopular* with the voters.]

un·pre·pared (un′ pri pard′) *adj.* not prepared or ready [We were *unprepared* for visitors.]

un·sat·is·fac·tor·y (un′ sat is fak′ tə rē) *adj.* not good enough to meet needs or wishes [Her work was *unsatisfactory*.] —**un′ sat·is·fac′ tor·i·ly** *adv.*

un·sel·fish (un sel′ fish) *adj.* not selfish; putting the good of others before one's own interests [His *unselfish* act was admired by others.] —**un·self′ ish·ly** *adv.*

un·til (un til′) *prep.* up to the time of [Don't leave *until* noon.] ♦*conj.* to the point that [She ate *until* she was full.]

un·u·su·al (un yoo′ zhoo wəl) *adj.* not usual or common. —**un·u′ su·al·ly** *adv.*

un·wel·come (un wel′ kəm) *adj.* not wanted [That rude person is *unwelcome* here.]

use·ful (yoos′ fəl) *adj.* that can be used [A can opener is a *useful* tool.] —**use′ ful·ly** *adv.*

V

va·ca·tion (və kā′ shən *or* vā kā′ shən) *n.* a period of time when one stops working to rest [They went to Mexico on *vacation*.] —*pl.* **va·ca′ tions** ♦*v.* to take one's vacation [We *vacationed* at home this summer.] —**va·ca′ tioned, va·ca′ tion·ing**

vi·ta·min (vīt′ ə min) *n.* any of certain substances needed by the body to keep healthy. —*pl.* **vi′ ta·mins**

voice (vois) *n.* sound made through the mouth, especially in talking [His *voice* was loud.] —*pl.* **voic′ es**

vote (vōt) *v.* to show one's decision on something by marking a ballot or raising a hand [We *voted* for club president.] —**vot′ ed, vot′ ing**

voy·age (voi′ ij) *n.* a journey by water [They went on a *voyage* around the world.] —*pl.* **voy′ ag·es**

W

wait·er (wāt′ ər) *n.* a man who waits on tables. —*pl.* **wait′ ers**

wait·ress (wā′ tris) *n.* a woman who waits on tables in restaurants. —*pl.* **wait′ ress·es**

waste·ful (wāst′ fəl) *adj.* using more than needed [Some *wasteful* people throw away good food.] —**waste′ ful·ly** *adv.*

weath·er (we*th*′ ər) *n.* the conditions outside at a particular time [We had nice *weather* today.]

we'd (wēd) we would; we had.

weigh (wā) *v.* to use scales to find out how heavy a thing is [She *weighed* the package at the post office.] —**weighed, weigh′ ing**

weight (wāt) *n.* **1** the heaviness of something [Many people worry about their *weight*.] **2** any unit of heaviness such as a pound, kilogram, etc.

when's (hwenz) when is.

where's (hwerz) where is.

wheth·er (hwe*th*′ ər) *conj.* if it is true or likely that [I don't know *whether* I can go.]

who'll (hōōl) who will.

wide (wīd) *adj.* great in width [The street is *wide*.] —**wid′ er, wid′ est** —**wide′ ly** *adv.*

wild (wīld) *adj.* **1** living or growing in nature; not tamed or used for farming, etc. by human beings. **2** rough, not controlled, reckless [He had a *wild* plan to get rich quickly.] —**wild′ ly** *adv.*

wise·ly (wīz′ lē) *adv.* in an informed or learned way; in a way that shows good judgment [He *wisely* decided to remain silent.]

witch (wich) *n.* a woman imagined to have magic power. —*pl.* **witch′ es**

wom·an (woom′ ən) *n.* an adult, female human being. —*pl.* **wom′ en**

won·der·ful (wun′ dər fəl) *adj.* that causes wonder; marvelous; amazing.

won't (wōnt) will not.

wood·en (wood′ 'n) *adj.* made of wood.

work·man (wʉrk′ mən) *n.* a worker; laborer. —*pl.* **work′ men**

wor·ry (wʉr′ ē) *v.* to feel or make uneasy or troubled [His sadness *worried* us.] —**wor′ ried, wor′ ry·ing**

would (wood) *v.* a helping verb used in speaking of something that depends on something else, or in asking something in a polite way [She *would* have agreed if you'd waited. *Would* you please repeat that?]

wouldn't (wood′ 'nt) would not.

wres·tle (res′ 'l) *v.* to struggle with, trying to throw or force to the ground [The boys *wrestled* until they fell.] —**wres′ tled, wres′ tling**

Y

yawn (yôn) *v.* to breathe deeply in an uncontrolled manner, as when one is tired [She *yawned* at bedtime.] —**yawned, yawn′ ing**

yield (yēld) *v.* to give the right of way to [*Yield* to traffic at the next corner.] —**yield′ ed, yield′ ing**

you'd (yōōd) you would; you had.

a	fat	**ir**	here	**ou**	out	**zh**	leisure
ā	ape	**ī**	bite, fire	**u**	up	**ng**	ring
ä	car, lot	**ō**	go	**ʉr**	fur		a *in* ago
e	ten	**ô**	law, horn	**ch**	chin		e *in* agent
er	care	**oi**	oil	**sh**	she	**ə** = i *in* unity
ē	even	**oo**	look	**th**	thin		o *in* collect
i	hit	**ōō**	tool	**th**	then		u *in* focus

Lesson 1

vi

serving

inviting

Lesson 2

try

completely

closely

sincerely

bravely

Lesson 3

le

ageless

homeless

shapeless

tireless

Lesson 4

br

bread

break

Lesson 5

oi

foil

coin

joint

voice

Lesson 6

wo

won't

wouldn't

Lesson 7

ei

weigh

neighbor

receive

ceiling

Lesson 10

ys

subways

holidays

chimneys

highways

Lesson 11

rl

curlier

curliest

earlier

earliest

Lesson 12

yi

trying

denying

replying

worrying

wn

lawn

dawn

yawned

wl

shawl

crawling

gh

caught

taught

daughter

au

haunt

sauce

because

autumn

Lesson 15

ow

howl

power

clown

flower

Lesson 16

ou

though

should

dough

enough

Lesson 19

bi

scrubbing

grabbing

Lesson 20

ps

clips

snaps

op

hoped

hopped

ge

dodge

edge

sponge

garage

wi

witch

sandwich

re

future

picture

nature

mixture

po

unpopular

unimportant

mi

mislead

misspell

misprint

misunderstand

ot

pilot

pilot's

or

doctors

doctors'

sailors

sailors'

Lesson **32**

bl

double

table

marble

Lesson **33**

on

action

question

invention

caution

Lesson **34**

nt

basement

pavement

amusement

excitement

Tara's school soccer team has lost many games recently. All the students are feeling disappointed. Tara has written a school team cheer to lift everyone's spirits. Mark her errors in grammar, capitalization, punctuation, and spelling. Then correct her errors as you make a clean copy of her school cheer on your own paper.

Never Say Die!

Central Coyotes never say die!

With tireless spirit, we give it a try.

Our games are never boreing.

We aim to keep on scoring.

When our Foes think we are weak,

We turn up the heat and start to streek.

A nosefull of dust just makes us fight.

Its usless to block us, try as you might.

Bravley we charge. what is defeet.

Wisely we play. we wont be beat.

Central coyotes never say die!

We're reddy and able to give our best try

Your Turn   Imagine that you have been chosen to write a new team cheer for your school. You might want to praise the team for a good job, or you might want to urge the team to keep trying. In your cheer try to use as many silent **e** words with the endings **ing** and **ly, ful** and **less** as you can. Then proofread your work.

Michael was assigned to cover the Coyotes' game for the school newspaper. He had quite a surprise. He wrote a paragraph to tell what happened at the game. Mark Michael's errors in grammar, capitalization, punctuation, and spelling. Then correct his errors as you make a clean copy of his paragraph on your own paper.

Coyotes Win by a Song

By Michael Isaacs

The noysemakers were silent. The fans was used to defeat. They already knew this might be the Coyote's eghth loss in a row. The game was tied, and niether goalie had yeilded a score in several minutes. Then the most unlikley thing happened   Julie jackson stood up in front of the bleechers and began to sing   In a forcefull voyce she sang, "Were not spineless   Let's win this game! Her words pierced the silence. Soon the fans had learned the words to Julies' original tune and were joyning in. Just seconds remained. It was an exciteing finish. The Coyote's avoyded defeat by one point. Can they do it again next week.

Your Turn   Think of an exciting game or match you have seen. It might be a school game, a professional game, or just a game with friends. Write a paragraph that tells what happened. Use as many **ie** and **ei** words as you can. Then proofread your work, paying special attention to words spelled with **ea** and **oi.**

Proofreading Practice

Lessons 10–13   Captions

Julio took many pictures of Rocky Mountain National Park in Colorado when he went there on vacation with his family. Julio wants to remember every moment of his exciting trip, so he has prepared some detailed captions for the photographs in his album. Mark his errors in grammar, capitalization, punctuation, and spelling. Then correct his errors as you make a clean copy of his captions on your own paper.

This road goes straight up! It is called Old Fall river road. Going down was the easyest part.

These ponys were easy to ride. We are at Timber creek campground, and we liked picking blueberrys. A fawn is hidden in the bushes at the edge of the stream we didn't see the mother.

There are no grizzlies in the park this is a black bear. The bear didn't pay no attention to us. My sister was really worryed though.

We got up at dawn to see this deer. We also spotted a hawwk. Earlyest I had ever gotten up in my life!

This beaver is carrying a branch across a beaver dam. I watched him crawl through a hole in the dam. Beavers seem busyer than other animals. Now I know what the term "eager beaver" means!

Your Turn   Think of photographs or objects from trips you have taken. Write a caption for a photograph or a description of a souvenir you especially like. Try to use as many words as you can that are plurals of final **y** words or **consonant + y** words with the ending **er, est, ing,** or **ed.** Also include words spelled with **aw.** Proofread your work.

Julio and his family saw some wonderful sights on their vacation. Julio sent a postcard to a friend, describing his favorite activities. Mark his errors in grammar, capitalization, punctuation, and spelling. Then correct his errors as you make a clean copy of his description on your own paper.

Dear Chris,

Rocky Mountain national Park is really awesome! Its a giant mountain playgrond Today we went hiking along trails that the Arapaho used thousands of years ago. We were surronded by beautiful streams, wildflouers, meadows, and vallies. I didn't see any waterfalls. I did see a mountain goat thowgh   he was standing all by himself on a bolder just above the trail. After our hike we went fishing and I caught three rainbow trout! This been one of the happyest days of my life!

See you soon,

Julio

Your Turn   Think of a wonderful place that you have seen. It might be a place near your home or a place you have seen on a trip. Write a description of that place. Use as many words as you can that have the **au, ou,** and **ow** letter patterns you learned in Lessons 14–16. Then proofread your work.

Proofreading Practice

Lessons 19–22   Riddles

Rhonda loves riddles. She has written a page of riddles to stump her friends. Mark Rhonda's errors in grammar, capitalization, punctuation, and spelling. Then correct her errors as you make a clean copy of the riddles on your own paper.

Q. Why did the baby goat nudg his mother?

A. He was a little kidder.

Q. Why did the light bulb shine dimmly?

A. The plugs saped its energy.

Q. Why did the athlete stop being forgettful?

A. he jogged his memory.

Q. Why was the cornstalk scard

A. He was afraid to have his ears trimmed

Q. Why was the rosebush bragging about her son?

A. He was a buding genius.

Q. How do you know that Electricity is musical?

A. You can hear it humming in the wires

Q. Why did the butter knife have to skipp recess?

A. He was cutting up in class.

Q. Why did the inventor keep tapping the edje of his hat?

A. It was briming with ideas.

Your Turn   Think of some clever riddles to stump your friends and family. Use as many **1 + 1 + 1** words and silent **e** words with endings as you can. Then proofread your work.

Many riddles answer the question *why.* Longer forms of writing can also explain why. When Leroy's class was studying about different kinds of jobs, Leroy decided to write a paragraph about why he wanted to become a clown. Mark Leroy's mistakes in grammar, capitalization, punctuation, and spelling. Then correct his mistakes as you make a clean copy of his paragraph on your own

Staring as a clown would be the greatest job in the

World. First, there is the advenchure of traveling from

town to town. There is also the fun of putting on an

orang wig huuge shoes and a sponge ball for a nose.

In some circuses clowns gladley help pich the tent and

feed the animals. They also take chancs on the high

wire in addition to doing funny stunts. in one circus

some clowns rides miniachure horses one of the

clowns keeps hoping from one horse to another. The

best part of a clown's job is hearing the audience

claping after they have watched the show.

Your Turn   What kind of job would you like to have? Think about what you would like to do for a living, and write a paragraph explaining why you would choose that job. Try to use words ending in **ch, tch,** and **ture.** Proofread your paragraph, paying special attention to plural forms.

This summer, for the first time, Theo will help out at his family's restaurant during the lunch hour. Each day Theo must write the lunch menu on a large chalkboard that all the customers can see. Mark Theo's errors in grammar, capitalization, punctuation, and spelling. Then correct his errors as you make a clean copy of the menu on your own paper.

Menu

Soups   Cup $1.25   Bowl $2.50

Creamy Mushroom

(Try this even if you disslike mushrooms its unnbelievably good!)

Black Bean

(Do you enjoy a little spice.   Our Cooks' seasoning is perfect.)

Salads

Seven Sea's Delights $4.50

(Crab lobster and shrimp are fresh from the atlantic ocean.)

Chef's Surprise $3.50

(Make no misstake. You should be very hungry when you order this.)

Desserts

(Everyone agrees that they're all good but everyone disagrees about which one is best A meal is incomplete without dessert.)

Aunt Ellas' Peach Pie $1.50

(sweet georgia peaches are an unusual treat. Top your's with ice cream.)

Double Dutch Delight $1.75

(The brownies, ice cream, and fudge sauce won't dissappoint you.)

Childrens' menu available.

Your Turn   Imagine that you have been chosen to plan the menu for a family get-together. You can ask family members to bring favorite dishes or ones that they prepare especially well. As you write your menu, give each dish a name based on the relative who will prepare it, such as Uncle Burt's Barbequed Ribs. Use capital letters for the name of each dish, and be careful to spell correctly all singular and plural possessive forms. Then proofread your menu.

Theo wanted to share some interesting news about his summer job, so he wrote a letter to his friend Joshua. Mark Theo's errors in grammar, capitalization, punctuation, and spelling. Then correct his errors as you make a clean copy of his letter on your own paper.

August 10, 19—

Dear Joshua,

I'm working in my familys' restaurant this summer. Yesterday at noon we had some unnexpected excitement there was a terribel thunderstorm. Suddenly the lights was out and our kitchen was in total darknness. Dad thought of a solushun and put candels both in the kitchen and on all the diner's tables. Even with the candels there was some missunderstanding, and a few of the waitresses' orders got mixed up. Two childrens' hamburgers had pickels and onions that had not been ordered. One womans' salad was chicken instead of tuna. Finally the lights came back on. Dad gave everyone triple brownie treats for free because we dont want any unhappy or displeased customers. Was a long lunch hour!

Your friend,

Theo

Your Turn   What news do you have that you can share in a letter? Think of someone who would like to hear from you, and write to that person. Try to include some words that end with a consonant followed by **le.** Then as you proofread your work, look for words that end with **ment** or **ness.** See if you spelled those words correctly.

ILLUSTRATIONS
Shirley Beckes: 30, 35, 84, 86, 87, 90, 99, 102, 108, 109, 110, 111
Gwen Connelly: 7, 52, 53, 55, 57, 65, 69, 76, 122, 137, 138, 139, 145, 146
David Cunningham: 5
Ray Fredericks: 5, 83
Martucci Studio/Jerry Malone: 6
Diana Magnuson: 8, 12, 16, 20, 24, 28, 32, 36, 169, 171, 172, 173, 174, 175, 176, 177, 178, 179, 180, 181, 182, 183, 184, 185, 186, 187, 188, 189, 190, 191, 192, 193, 194, 195, 196, 197, 199
Ed Atchison: 9, 10, 11, 13, 15, 18, 19, 23, 26, 29, 34, 38, 39, 115
Troy Thomas: 45
George Suyeoka: 46, 50, 54, 58, 62, 66, 70, 74
Joe Veno: 47, 60, 61, 63, 67, 68, 72, 75, 117
George Ulrich: 85, 94, 95, 97, 101, 103, 106, 107, 113, 114
Yoshi Miyake: 88, 92, 96, 100, 104, 112
William P. Kaufmann: 121
Larry Frederick: 124, 125, 127, 128, 131, 135, 141, 143, 144, 147, 148, 149, 153
B. J. Johnson: 126, 130, 134, 142, 150

COVER: Design, Peter D. Reid
       Photography, John Morrison, Morrison Photography